ALLERGEN FREE

Baking

baked treats for all occasions

by Jill Robbins

Published by Family Matters Publishing, NH
Printed in the United States of America

This book is lovingly dedicated to my son, Bradley.

Published in the United States of America by Family Matters Publishing.
Printed in the United States of America.

Cover and Diagram Designer: Jan Streitburger
Cover Photographer: Larry Dunn
Section Divider Artist: Bradley Robbins

Library of Congress Control Number: 2007901605
Robbins, Jill
      Allergen Free Baking: Baked Treats for All Occasions/by Jill Robbins
      Includes index
      ISBN 10: **0-9776836-1-3**
      ISBN 13: **978-0-9776836-1-1** paperback

Table of Contents

Amaranth=Am
Barley = Ba
Buckwheat = Bu
Corn = Co
Quinoa = Qu
Rice = Ri (besides rice milk)
Spelt (note: spelt is in the wheat family) = Sp
Sorghum = So
Oats (note: oats in the USA may contain traces of wheat) = Oa
Can be prepared Gluten Free = GF
Can be prepared GF if flour bag is labeled that way (see p. 3) = GF*
Little or no white sugar = LNS
Optional alternative to other grain = ( )

Recipes by Type of Treat

Snack Bars and Brownies: 51

Cookies: 57

Cake and Ice Cream: 87

Acknowledgments

Thank you to all the friends, acquaintances, and even strangers, who have been so willing to sample and provide feedback throughout this process. Thank you in particular to all those children who let me know how happy they felt when getting to eat these treats. One of those children, Brianna Carter, now graces the back cover of the cookbook.

Most of all, thanks to my family. For the first several years of my baking efforts, they supported me with their humor and appreciation. When my efforts started paying off with good results, their encouragement, and that of others, resulted in my starting this cookbook. Over the three years of developing the recipes for this book, my family has taste-tested every final recipe, and often many of the multiple versions. Thanks to my husband, Phil, who always helped ensure that I would have the time I needed to bake. Special thanks to my son, Bradley, who throughout has been my inspiration.

Forward

If you asked me five or six years ago whether we could possibly assemble the kinds of wonderful-tasting, organic treats we are now offering, I would have laughed. Jill had been laboring intensively to find treats for our son, who like millions of children, suffered from various food allergies. Jill finally decided to try creating her own treats. She had had some experience in graduate school conducting research, so it was not a huge leap for her to use our son and me as guinea pigs for her various creations. Unfortunately, those early concoctions didn't exactly make us salivate like Pavlov's research dogs. My son and I had lots of fun at Jill's expense, teasing her about her latest offerings. In our hearts, though, we hoped each one would be good; after all, she was working hard so that our son would be able to have treats like all the other kids.

I'm not sure I can pinpoint when it was exactly, but I vividly remember the first time she handed our son and me a peach muffin that tasted like… well, it tasted like a peach muffin! My son and I were stunned and thrilled; our eyes widened and our jaws dropped, although we soon closed them again on a second helping. A new family rating scale emerged that we use to this day. My son and I rate Jill's products on a scale from 1 to 100. We are harsh critics and the treats must hit in the nineties to be considered as a Gak Snack. We trust you will agree.

Phil Robbins

Introduction

This cookbook is for the novice baker and the experienced baker. It is for anyone who wants to bake a special treat for someone with a food allergy, a treat that will be so delicious that other people will want to eat it too.

For families with a food allergic member, special occasions have posed unique challenges. This cookbook is designed to help. It is organized not only by type of treat, but also by special occasion – be it a birthday, a holiday, or a school party. The recipes are for the treats common to each occasion: birthday cakes for birthdays; pumpkin pie, apple pie, and cornbread for Thanksgiving; cookies, brownies, and cupcakes for a school party.

Most of the recipes in this book use fruit and/or fruit juice, many use at least some whole grain, and none contain peanuts, tree nuts, egg, wheat, dairy, cholesterol, or trans fat. Soy lecithin is the only soy ingredient. Seeds are in only two recipes, as optional items. The recipes call for a range of flours, and some of the recipes are gluten free. Although in our baking facility we do not use spelt because people with true wheat allergies will be allergic to it, this cookbook offers many recipes with this wonderfully light and flavorful grain for those who are sensitive to wheat but are fine with spelt.

In order to achieve desserts that look, feel, and taste similar to "regular" desserts, these recipes contain some ingredients that may be unfamiliar, and use some methods that are slightly different from those in traditional cookbooks. With regard to the ingredients, once you have them stocked in your kitchen, you will find that they become easy and natural to use. For those who don't live near a health food store, we have made the more difficult to locate ingredients available on the Gak's Snacks web site, www.gakssnacks. com. Those concerned about trace amounts of allergens in ingredients may also be interested to know that the ingredients available from Gak's Snacks have been selected only from facilities that report excellent practices with regard to allergen cross contamination. Additionally, many have been tested in our facility for peanuts, almonds, eggs, and milk. With regard to the methods, almost every recipe follows the same basic procedure. That means that once you have made one treat, it will be simple to make most of them! For almost every recipe, all you will do is: Mix dry ingredients and sift 3 times, blend wet ingredients in blender, fold wet into dry, and bake. Simple!

Enjoy making, and eating, these creations!

Ingredient Notes

Many of the ingredients used in this cookbook are quite basic. However, some have details worth noting.

Baking powder: As with all the Gak's Snacks' ingredients, we chose our baking powder based on the allergen care reported by the manufacturer. The baking powder producer we selected makes only double acting baking powder. Therefore, all the recipes in this cookbook use double acting baking powder.

Chocolate Chips: "Chocolate chips" in this cookbook means "semi-sweet" chocolate chips, since "milk" chocolate is made with milk. For those who are concerned about traces of food allergens, Gak's Snacks web store (www. gakssnacks.com) offers chocolate chips and cocoa powder that are made and packaged in a dedicated facility with no peanuts, tree nuts, or wheat. Further, these products are *not* run on shared lines with dairy.

Cocoa Powder: Cocoa powder can be Dutched or natural. Dutched has been treated with alkaline chemicals to create a less acidic powder. The products in this book were developed with natural cocoa powder. If using Dutched, you may want to decrease sugar by about 1 Tbsp per cup, since Dutched cocoa powder is slightly sweeter than natural.

Fiber - whole grain versus white flour: Some whole grain flours, such as oats and barley, have great texture. Others, such as whole spelt and rice, can sometimes result in a heavier, grainier treat. For the recipes most likely to be shared with other kids, such as birthday cakes, we have included more white flour. Particularly to the allergic child, it can be an emotionally positive experience to have other children like and want the treats he/she is sharing. On the other hand, many of the recipes in this cookbook call for whole grain flour, which is much higher in fiber and nutrients than white flour. For recipes you'll be serving just to the family or close friends, you might want to experiment with increasing the proportion of whole grain to white. To increase the fiber content further, you might try replacing a tablespoon or two of white flour with an equal amount of oat bran or rice bran. These adjustments will work best in recipes for hearty foods, such as muffins and quick breads.

Fruit: As a general rule, it's always useful to taste fruit before cooking with it. If it tastes good, cook with it; otherwise, don't! What you bake will only taste as good as the ingredients you use.

Bananas: Try to use bananas that are nicely spotted. Too much brown and the taste will be off; any green and the banana will have limited sweetness.

If you have extra bananas that are perfectly ripe, try peeling and freezing them. In a crunch, these bananas can be used as baking ingredients when you are short on ripe bananas. To do this, leave the banana out for a couple of minutes to partially thaw. Then slice into thin slices to thaw fully, and proceed as usual.

Pears: Bartlett pears are sweet and juicy, and do well as a "wet ingredient". Use them when they smell sweet, when gentle finger pressure leaves an indent, and of course, when a taste test confirms that they are delicious! Bosc pears keep their shape and firmness nicely, so they do well in recipes in which you want actual pear pieces in the final product. Unlike most baking fruit, Bosc pears remain firm even when ripe. Instead of testing ripeness with finger pressure, monitor the color of the fruit. A ripe Bosc pear has brown, rather than yellow, skin.

Peaches: Peaches make great additions to baked goods. They can be used fresh or frozen. If using fresh peaches, try to avoid using much of the red part that touches the pit, since that section is slightly bitter.

Berries: To dry recently washed berries, try pouring them into a paper towel-lined bowl and rolling them around.

Oat Flour, Buckwheat flour, and Quinoa Flour: For those needing to bake **gluten-free**, please note that these flours can at times contain traces of wheat due to cross contamination in the field and in processing. However, they are becoming increasingly available wheat and gluten free; just be sure to look for a gluten free label on the package.

Safflower oil: Safflower oil is not always as available as other oils. Other oils such as corn, canola, sunflower, or soy oil can be substituted.

Soy lecithin: Lecithin can be made from soy or egg. Be sure to use *soy* lecithin. These recipes call for soy lecithin powder because it distributes well through a batter, and because it fits through a sifter. However, soy lecithin granules are fine as well. If you use granules, always mix them with the wet, rather than dry, ingredients, since they will not fit well through the sifter with the dry ingredients. Most, though not all, people with soy allergies are fine with soy lecithin because most of the protein has been removed. However, if you are baking for someone who has a soy allergy, be sure to ask if soy lecithin is okay. If not, feel free to leave it out, replacing it with the same amount of oil. The texture won't be quite as good, but the recipe will still come out well.

Spelt flour: Spelt is a form of wheat. Those with a true wheat allergy (as opposed to a wheat sensitivity) will also be allergic to spelt, and therefore will want to select alternative flours. For those who are completely fine with wheat, wheat can be used in place of spelt if desired.

Sugar: Most of the recipes in this cookbook call for "sugar." I developed the recipes using organic dried cane juice crystals, which is a thick, minimally processed natural sugar. You can use white cane sugar for any of the recipes, or give organic dried cane juice crystals a try. Sometimes sugar gets clumpy, especially brown or powdered sugar. For brown sugar, it is best to start with a new, soft sugar, because the recipe assumes the moisture. However, if you need to use the drier brown sugar in your cupboard, you can blend it briefly in the blender to get rid of any clumps. For powdered sugar, break up the largest clumps with a fork, measure it for the recipe, and then run it through a sifter.

Thickeners: The names **"tapioca starch"** and **"tapioca flour"** are used interchangeably. Similarly, the names **"arrowroot starch," "arrowroot flour,"** and **"arrowroot powder"** are used interchangeably. However, note that **"potato starch"** is **NOT** the same product as **"potato flour."** Potato flour is heavy, and typically is used for cooking. For baking, always use potato **starch**, which helps keep a baked product light. **Agar agar** is a type of sea weed used for gelling liquids. All of these thickeners can be found at health food stores.

Wheat flour and other substitutions: Many people using this cookbook are not baking for anyone with a wheat allergy. I have had many parents using a prior version of this cookbook ask if they can use wheat in all of the recipes. I have other customers telling me that they do use wheat in all of the recipes, and that it works well. What I would suggest with regard to wheat and any other substitution is to try the recipe first the way it is written, so you know how it is intended. Then experiment in whatever way you would ike - using wheat, leaving out the lecithin, reducin the sugar, adding bran, using soy milk, adding chocolate chips, or whatever other ideas you have. With regard to wheat use, the substitution should work perfectly with the recipes calling for spelt. For other recipes, keep in mind that wheat absorbs a bit more liquid than most other grains. Therefore, you might want to add a bit of liquid (e.g. 1 Tbsp water) if using wheat.

Xanthan gum: Xanthan gum is one of the few gums considered safe and natural enough to be allowed for organic baking. The combination of xanthan gum, lecithin powder, and tapioca starch allows great egg-free baking. If you decide to do your own experimentation with recipes, however, do not greatly increase the amount of xanthan gum, since very large amounts can lead to digestive difficulties. A bag of this item may seem expensive to purchase, but it actually costs only a few cents per recipe. A teaspoonful at a time goes a long way!

Making a Welcoming Baking Space

Starting a baking project can feel like an overwhelming task, or it can feel like a fun, relaxing, creative opportunity. Here are some tips to help baking feel like a breeze. The theme is: Set things up to avoid the hassles!

Setting up the kitchen:
"Ugh! I need a teaspoon of baking powder, but my measuring spoon is wet from vanilla extract." Though it is not a big deal to rinse and dry the spoon, I like hassle free baking. To avoid this particular hassle, these recipes suggest measuring dry ingredients before wet ones. Still, if you want to treat yourself to particularly easy baking, buy two sets of measuring spoons and measuring cups – one for dry ingredients and one for wet ones.
"Now where did I put the cinnamon?" "I know the lecithin is in here somewhere."
Arrange your space so that you no longer have to search for each ingredient each time you bake. Set aside a small accessible area in the freezer (for extending shelf life) for flour you expect to use only occasionally. Choose a section of the refrigerator and stock it with flour you use regularly, as well as lecithin powder (or granules) and maple syrup. Also select a spot in the refrigerator for opened containers of apple sauce, apple juice, lemon juice, rice milk (original flavor - i.e., not vanilla or chocolate), and safflower oil, and have an area in the cupboard for those products unopened. Choose another area in the cupboard and stock it with arrowroot powder, baking powder, baking soda, cinnamon, cloves, ginger, nutmeg, salt, vanilla extract, xanthan gum, canned pears, tapioca starch, potato starch, old fashioned oat flakes, honey, molasses, sugar, brown sugar, and powdered sugar. Finally, it can be handy to have plastic resealable bags for storage, and stickers for labeling them. With these basic products ready and waiting, you will be well prepared to bake anytime.

When ready to bake:
Set out a "dry ingredient" dinner plate, with a fork, a flat edged knife, and a set of measuring spoons and measuring cups. Near your blender, arrange a "wet ingredient" dinner plate with a fork, a soft spatula, and if you have them, the second set of measuring spoons and measuring cups. Set out a flour sifter and two large mixing bowls. For most recipes in this book, you'll now be ready with all the tools you'll need. If you keep the used utensils/cups on the plate, clean up will be easy.

Baking Basics and Tips

Some people using this cookbook have been baking for years. Many others, however, may have never done much baking before. Necessity sometimes makes great bakers. Even if you have never baked before, you can achieve success. It won't be long before you see your child, and yes, even your child's friends, smile while eating your creations. For those who are not experienced bakers, here are a few baking basics to assist you in the process.

Ingredient temperature: With the exception of cookie dough and pie crust, which are typically best chilled, most batter bakes best if the ingredients are at room temperature.

Measuring ingredients: I rarely measure ingredients when I cook meals, and if I do measure, it is almost never carefully. With baking, it's a different story altogether. The tiniest alterations really do affect the outcome of the recipe. So, don't estimate. Use measuring spoons and measuring cups. For dry ingredients, use the flat edge of a knife to smooth across the rim of the measuring spoon or cup so that the dry ingredient goes no higher (or lower) than the rim. When measuring flour for these recipes, use the measuring cup to scoop the flour out of the flour bag. (Scooping flour into a cup packs in more flour than spooning or pouring the flour into the cup.) Measure flour the way it comes in the package – i.e., do not pack it down into the measuring cup. In contrast, do pack down brown sugar and fruit. If any other ingredients are to be packed tightly into the measuring cup, the recipe will indicate that. When measuring maple syrup, honey, or molasses, use the measuring cup for oil first. Then the sweetener will slide right out! You might notice that the order of ingredients in some of these recipes puts oil right before the sweetener, for that very reason. Finally, with wet ingredients in general, be sure to use a spatula to scrape as much liquid as you reasonably can off the sides of the blender or bowl, to include it in the dough.

Using electric beaters: When ready to stop, reduce speed to the lowest, and then very slowly raise beaters out of batter. Excess batter will come off the beaters and drop back into the mixture.

Using a blender: Put wet ingredients directly into the blender - no extra bowls to wash! When you are done with the blender, turn the speed back to low so you don't start it on high by mistake later (leading to splattering). When ready to clean up, put a bit of dish soap and some warm water into the blender and blend it on low for a few seconds. The blender will be easy to clean after that! After you wash your blender components, dry the blades to prevent rusting.

Greasing a pan: For quick, mess-free, even greasing, try using an oil spray over the sink.

Flouring a pan: Put a tablespoon or so of flour into the oiled pan. Tip the pan at an angle and tap the sides to spread the flour, turning the pan and tapping until the sides and bottom all have a dusting of flour. To loosen and remove excess flour, try hitting the pan firmly while holding it upside down over the sink or garbage. If you are using two pans, try hitting the pans against each other.

Adding and maintaining air: Baking without eggs and wheat can result in heavy products. One way to help have lighter products is to add air. Most of the recipes in this cookbook therefore call for three techniques: Triple sifting, use of a blender, and folding of batter.

    Triple sifting: Triple sifting is sifting the dry ingredients three times. Although most of the air is added in the first sifting, the additional siftings can help a little. Furthermore, they help ensure that the other ingredients that help with lightness are evenly dispersed throughout the batter.

    Blending: Whipping the wet ingredients on the highest setting in a blender not only affects the texture of the batter, but also adds air bubbles into the wet ingredients.

    Folding: Most baked treats are best with the least possible handling. Once you have poured the wet into the dry ingredients, mix as little and as gently as possible - just until there is only an occasional drop of flour showing. Folding the batter is a technique in which you use a spatula to turn over batter from the bottom and sides of the bowl onto the top of the batter. It's kind of like slowly and carefully turning over pancakes, repeatedly. This gentle treatment will help to retain the air added from sifting and blending.

Timing: As long as the wet and dry ingredients are separate, you can take your time. Once you mix them, however, the clock is ticking (except for most cookies). The more quickly the food gets into the oven, the better it is likely to come out. As much as possible, aim for under 2 minutes (though a bit longer is usually okay) from when you mix the wet and dry ingredients until you get the food into the oven. It helps to check the recipe before mixing to make sure you have done any needed preparation: Are the dry ingredients sifted? Have you measured any "additional" ingredients that get added in at the last minute after partial mixing? Is the oven pre-heated? Is the pan greased? Did you get your child whatever is needed so you won't be interrupted for two or three minutes? If so, you'll be able to do the final steps smoothly and quickly.

Baking: Make sure that the oven is pre-heated completely before putting the food into the oven. When possible, bake on the middle rack, and on only one rack at a time. Allow at least an inch of space around any pan to allow good air flow. If you need to use a pan size different from the one recommended, adjust cooking time accordingly (longer for a smaller pan, shorter for a larger pan).

Hopefully your child will feel like jumping up and down in eager and excited anticipation of getting to try the treat baking in the oven. But while a muffin, bread, or cake is in the oven, try to help the excitement be expressed in ways other than literal jumping and running. If you can feel the floor move from your child's activities, your creation in the oven can feel it too. All that air you added to it with the sifting and blending gives lightness to your treats, but a good bump on the floor can pop that air right out!

Once the food is in the oven, leave the oven door closed until you believe the food is fully cooked. This is especially important with cakes. If the food needs more time, determine that quickly so that the door is open as briefly as possible. Most items are done when they are slightly browned. You can also check, with muffins and cakes, by pushing down slightly on the surface with a finger and then releasing. If the cake springs back up, at least most of the way, the food is probably ready. You can also insert a toothpick. If it comes out clean, the food is probably ready.

Cooling: Baked treats need air around them to cool properly. Always let them sit on a cooling rack until they are completely cool.

Removing a cake from a pan: Place a plate over the top of the pan. Holding the plate and the pan, flip both over so that the cake falls into the plate. Repeat the process by putting a cooling rack on top of the plate. Flip both over, and the cake will be right side up on the cooling rack. To remove cupcakes and their paper cups from pans when soft, without compressing them or loosening the paper, try using a butter knife on one side, and fingers on the other.

Freezing:
Once fully cooled, most of the baked goods in this cookbook can be frozen! Of course, everyone will want to eat fresh that day some of what you have baked, and will want some saved for the following day's breakfast, lunch, or snack. But it's great also to have some that can go into the freezer for when you don't have time to bake. For an upcoming event, freeze items whole. For snacks and leftover birthday cake, freeze individual portion sizes. You may want to put each portion into its own labeled baggie or mini container in preparation for those times when you need to be on the go in a hurry. That way, when you need it, it is totally ready to go! If you do this with several different treats, then you can have a section of your freezer in which there is a nice selection of goodies. You can then easily vary what goes into the snack bag or lunchbox. Label the name of the treat, who the food is for (if not everyone!), and the date you baked it. Now you're ready for any occasion!

Baking with Kids

Lots of kids enjoy baking. For kids with food allergies, helping to bake can also be reassuring – they can see and control every ingredient that will be in the finished product.

A few especially fun recipes to make with children are: Garden Surprise, Raisindoras, Donuts, and Gingerbread People. You might also try a creative project: Design your own snack bar. Kids can have a great time selecting and mixing sticky ingredients (e.g. honey, dates, melted chocolate) and dry ingredients (e.g. flour, cold cereal, crumbled cookies) and being able to say, "I made this!"

Once the treat is in the oven, see if you can make it a game to get everything cleaned up before the treat comes out of the oven. That will be a particular challenge with the cookies, since they cook fast. If you succeed, then when the treat is ready to eat, all you have left to do is thoroughly enjoy it!

Food Preparation and Serving with Regard to Allergens

If you are reading this, either you or someone you care about probably has a food allergy. Your kitchen may be free of the relevant allergen(s), making it easy to avoid cross-contamination with the food allergen when baking. If the allergen or allergens are present in your kitchen, or if you are baking for a group - in which case someone may have an allergy to a substance that your family does not avoid - use every precaution when cooking to avoid cross-contamination. This includes particularly careful hand washing, disinfecting work spaces, and using care not to use shared utensils.

When serving, use similar care. If bringing your food to someone else's event, be sure the host or hostess knows to have "dedicated" serving utensils. Finally, if providing a treat for a group, such as at a pot luck or a bake sale, you might want to label the treat with a little sign (a small folded piece of card paper works great). That way, other people with allergies can read "Made with no nuts…" and enjoy the treat too.

Holidays and Other Occasions Made Easy

Food is central at many social occasions and holidays. Ideally, everyone can partake of the food together. In this section, you can find ideas for treats fitting each occasion, treats that can be shared and enjoyed by all. Of course, there is no need to limit yourself to these ideas. As you browse through the cookbook, you might light on others as well.

Breakfast

More so than lunch and dinner foods, most typical breakfast foods contain major food allergens – eggs, dairy, and wheat. For some with peanut or tree nut allergies, it can even be a challenge to find cold cereal, since most are made in facilities with nuts. But take cheer – below you will find a variety of delicious breakfast treats that you can serve at home, and also that you can take along when going out for breakfast:

Apple Buckwheat Pancakes 18
Blueberry Scokiemuffs 20
Donuts 22
French Toast 26
Granola 27
Cranberry Granola 28
Quick Pancakes 29
Quick Blueberry Pancakes 31
Quick Waffles 30
Quick Blueberry Waffles 30
Apple Oat Cereal Muffins 32
Apple Rice Cereal Muffins 34
Tea Hee Hee Cake 50
Cherry (or other fruit) Syrup 123

Morning play group

When it's time for the kids to get together, it is great when they can all enjoy the same treats. Here are some just right for a morning gathering:

Blueberry Scokiemuffs 20
Donuts 22
Apple Muffins 32
Apple Oat Cereal Muffins 33

Apple Rice Cereal Muffins 34
Blueberry Muffins 35
Carrot Spice Muffins and Bread 36
Chocolate Chip Banana Muffins 37
Cranberry Muffins 38
Peach Muffins 39
Banana Bread 41
Banana Rice Bread 42
Cranberry Bread 45
Wholesome Zucchini Carrot Bread 48
Zucchini Bread 49

Play Dates

Tip: Try keeping a supply of home-made frozen cookie dough in the freezer. When your child has a friend over, pop a few spoonfuls into the toaster oven on oiled aluminum foil. Fresh cookies will be ready a few minutes later, and with no messy clean-up! For other ideas, try:

Chocolate Brownies 54
Raisindoras 55
Banana Chip Cookies 58
Bunuelos 60
Chocolate Chip Cookies 63
Soft Chocolate Chocolate Chip Cookies 64
Crunchy Chocolate Chocolate Chip Cookies 67
Maple Raisin Cookies 80
Oatmeal Raisin Cookies 81
Sugar Cookies 84

School Snacks

Finding great snacks to send to school for snack and lunch time can be easy as pie. Actually, although pie isn't listed below because it is a bit harder to pack than the rest, it, too, can make a great snack. My son thinks it's great when I surprise him with a container of pumpkin pie, and I think it's great that he's getting all that Vitamin A. Here are some easy to pack ideas:

Apple Muffins 32
Apple Oat Cereal Muffins 33
Apple Rice Cereal Muffins 34
Blueberry Muffins 35
Carrot Rice Spice Muffins and Bread 36
Chocolate Chip Banana Muffins 37

Cranberry Muffins 38
Peach Muffins 39
Banana Bread 41
Banana Rice Bread 42
Cranberry Bread 45
Wholesome Zucchini Carrot Bread 48
Zucchini Bread 49
Apricot Oat Bars 52
Apricot Oat Trail Bars 53
Bradley Bars 53
Raisindoras 55
Sweet Cranberry Crisps 56
Banana Chip Cookies 58
Chocolate Chip Cookies 63
Soft Chocolate Chocolate Chip Cookies 64
Crunchy Chocolate Chocolate Chip Cookies 67
Ginger Cookies 75
Jam Cookies 79
Maple Raisin Cookies 80
Oatmeal Raisin Cookies 81
Vanilla Cookies 86
Sugar Cookies 84

School Party

Bringing in a tray of goodies for a school party and having other kids wanting more is a fantastic experience for a child with food allergies. Here are some likely big hits:

Chocolate Brownies 54
Banana Chip Cookies 58
Chocolate Chip Cookies 63
Soft Chocolate Chocolate Chip Cookies 64
Crunchy Chocolate Chocolate Chip Cookies 67
Maple Raisin Cookies 80
Oatmeal Raisin Cookies 81
Sugar Cookies/Decorated Cookies 84
Chocolate Cupcakes 90
Rich Chocolate Cupcakes 92
Valentine's Day Cake 113
Vanilla Cupcakes 94
Vanilla Pear Cupcakes 95
Yellow Cupcakes 96

Birthday Party

Some parents of children with food allergies are used to serving two birthday cakes, and sometimes two kinds of ice cream – one that the allergic child can eat, and one that the friends will like. They want their child to be able to have the food at his or her own birthday party, but don't think anyone else will find that food to be sufficiently appetizing. The following recipes ought to serve both functions, so that everyone can enjoy the same one cake. Some of the cakes are like "regular" cakes. Even the ones that are a bit different (the ones made with rice, for example), are sufficiently tasty to be served to non-allergic guests.

Eating Out

Having food allergies, particularly to wheat or dairy, typically precludes being able to eat the baked treats served at restaurants. At the start of the meal when everyone is hungry, the bread or crackers are likely to be off limits. At the end of the meal, those luscious desserts usually also contain allergens. Although the hurdle of baked treats at restaurants may seem insurmountable initially, it can actually become the easiest to resolve of all the restaurant issues: You can use this cookbook to prepare delicious substitutes to what the restaurant may offer! Freeze portion-sized pieces of your child's favorite fruit breads and desserts, with each portion in its own baggy. Then it will be simple to bring a portion of fruit bread to the restaurant as a tempting bread substitute. If your party might be getting dessert, bring a favorite dessert along from your freezer for your child. Cookies tend to be the easiest to transport, but packing a slice of pie or cake in a plastic container and cooler bag is also "a piece of cake".

Recommended treats to substitute for restaurant bread:
Apple Muffins 32
Blueberry Muffins 35
Carrot Rice Spice Muffins and Bread 36
Chocolate Chip Banana Muffins 37
Cranberry Muffins 38
Peach Muffins 39
Banana Bread 41
Banana Rice Bread 42
Corn Bread 43
Zucchini Carrot Corn Bread 44
Cranberry Bread 45
Wholesome Zucchini Carrot Bread 48
Zucchini Bread 49
Tea Hee Hee Cake 50

Recommended desserts to bring to restaurants:
Your child's favorites!

Athletic Activities
For the soccer field or a mountain trail, here are a few quick energy bars:
Apricot Oat Bars 52
Apricot Oat Trail Bars 53
Bradley Bars 53
Sweet Cranberry Crisps 56

Tea
These treats go great with tea, and are nice to serve to company as well.
Tea Hee Hee Cake 50
Raisindoras 55

Chocolate Wafer Cookies 68
Donut Cookies 70
Ginger Cookies 75
Jam Cookies 79
Vanilla Cookies 86

Entertaining/Pot Lucks

For more formal entertaining, try these:
Chocolate Brownies 54
Chocolate Jam Sandwich Cookies 68
Maple Raisin Cookies 80
Chocolate Fudge Cake 102
Glazed Blueberry Cake 106
Lemon Cake 107
Strawberry Shortcake 111
Vanilla Cake with Blueberry Peach Sauce 114
Vanilla Icing 121
Lemon Icing 121
Peach Cobbler 128
Upside-Down Pear Gingerbread 130
Blueberry Pie 137
Cherry Pie 138

Holidays

Wherever you spend the holidays, these treats can be enjoyed by all:
Valentine's Day
Valentine's Day Cake 113
Cherry Pie 138
Purim
Hamentashen 76
Easter
Easter Egg Cake 103
Passover
Peachy Passover Cookies 83
Halloween
Donuts 22
Donut Cookies 70
Pumpkin Muffins 40
Thanksgiving
Cranberry Muffins 38
Pumpkin Muffins 40

Key of Grains, Gluten, and Sugar

Amaranth=Am
Barley = Ba
Buckwheat = Bu
Corn = Co
Quinoa = Qu
Rice = Ri (besides rice milk)
Spelt = Sp (note, spelt is in the wheat family)
Sorghum = So
Oats = Oa
Can be prepared Gluten Free = GF
Can be prepared GF if flour bag is so labeled (see p. 3) = GF*
Little or no white sugar = LNS
Optional alternative to other grain = ( )

Recipes
By Type of Treat

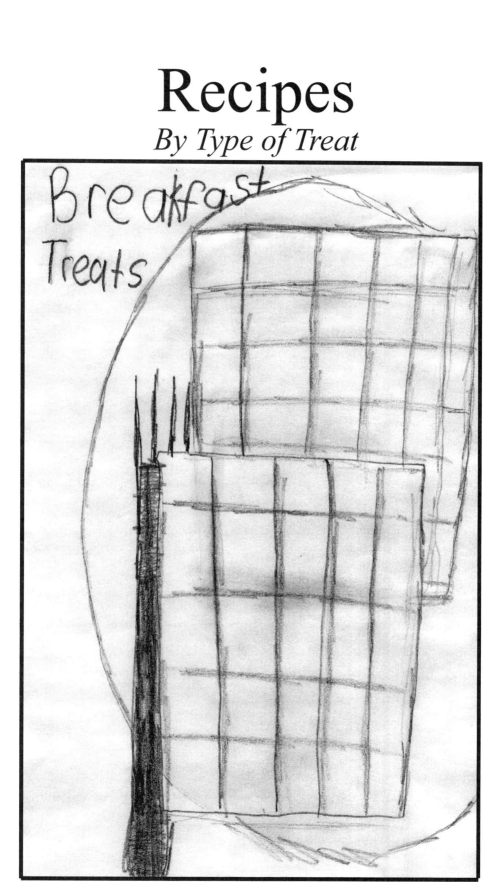

Apple Buckwheat Pancakes
(makes about 10 4" pancakes)

Dry Ingredients*:
1 1/8 c (1 c plus 2 Tbsp) barley flour*

1/3 cup buckwheat flour (Option, for a slightly lighter feel, you might want to replace the buckwheat flour with quinoa flour. It has a slightly - forgive me - "nutty" flavor. If so, add ½ tsp more cinnamon and ½ tsp more vanilla.)

2 Tbsp potato starch

2 Tbsp sugar

1 Tbsp tapioca starch

2 tsp cinnamon

1 tsp soy lecithin powder

1 tsp baking powder

½ tsp baking soda

½ tsp salt

Wet Ingredients:
1 c rice milk

1/3 c safflower oil

1/3 c water (room temperature or slightly warm)

2 Tbsp maple syrup (or for an interesting flavor, agave syrup!)

2 Tbsp apple juice

½ tsp vanilla extract

Extra Ingredients:
1 c chopped apples

Canola (or other) oil for cooking

Mix dry ingredients with a fork, then sift (optional) 1 time.

Put wet ingredients into blender (or, if short on time, skip this and just mix wet ingredients in a bowl). Blend on low for about 15 seconds and then on high for about 45 seconds.

Heat skillet on medium/low.

Pour wet into dry (gradually while mixing for gluten free), and stir with fork until almost mixed. (For gluten free, push clumps against side of bowl with back of fork to break up large clumps if needed).

Add apples, and stir until just mixed, stirring as little as possible.

Add oil to skillet. When the oil is hot enough so that a drop of batter dropped in it starts to sizzle or cook right away, pour in pancake batter of the size desired (for gluten free, small will be easier to flip). Tilt pan if needed to spread the pancake batter to an even thickness. Cover the pan loosely until the edges (outer ½ inch or so) of the pancakes are cooked and the batter in the middle is bubbling (For gluten free, keep covered longer and wait longer before flipping). It is ok to uncover the pan periodically to check on progress and to adjust temperature if needed to prevent burning. Then flip with a firm spatula, and cook uncovered until new bottom is lightly browned. For each new pancake, add a bit of oil to the pan. If the batter thickens too much, add a bit of water to the batter and stir with fork.

Serve with maple syrup, or with Cherry (or other fruit) Syrup (see page 123).

*For a delicious gluten free version, use wet ingredients as written except use 1 tsp vanilla instead of 1/2 tsp. Use dry ingredients as follows:
½ c quinoi flour
½ c white rice flour
1/3 cup buckwheat flour
¼ c potato starch
¼ c sugar
2 Tbsp tapioca starch
2 ½ tsp cinnamon
1 tsp soy lecithin powder
1 tsp baking powder
½ tsp baking soda
½ tsp salt
3/4 tsp xanthan gum

Blueberry Scokiemuffs
(makes 9 large scokiemuffs)

So, you want to know, "What IS a scokiemuff?" It's a wonderful combination of a scone, a cookie, and a muffin! It seemed a fitting name.

Pre-heat oven to 425°F. Oil 1 large cookie sheet, or use parchment paper.

Dry Ingredients:
1 1/8 c (1 c plus 2 Tbsp) barley flour
¾ c sugar
½ c oat flour
3 Tbsp plus 1 tsp potato starch
2 Tbsp tapioca flour
1 tsp cream of tartar
1 tsp soy lecithin powder
½ tsp baking soda
¼ tsp baking powder
½ tsp xanthan gum
¼ tsp salt

Wet Ingredients:
1/3 c canola oil
1/3 c ripe (or canned) peeled pear, chopped into large pieces
1/4 c rice milk
2 Tbsp lemon juice
1 Tbsp warm water

Extra Ingredients:
1 c fresh or frozen blueberries (if frozen, rinse to thaw, and pat at least somewhat dry)
1 – 2 tsp barley flour (only if using frozen berries)

Mix dry ingredients together, and sift 3 times.

Put wet ingredients in blender.

If using frozen blueberries, thaw by rinsing with cold water in colander or strainer. Then pat reasonably dry, sprinkle with the "extra ingredient" flour, and stir to coat the berries with the flour. If using fresh berries, wash and dry only.

Mix wet ingredients in blender on low for 15 seconds and on high for about a minute.

Pour wet into dry and fold gently until partially blended. Add blueberries and fold until barely blended. The batter will be light and soft yet almost rough looking. Use a large spoon to spoon onto cookie sheet.

Cook for 20 minutes, or until lightly browned.

Donuts
(makes 2 dozen small donuts -
Fun for a rainy October day)

Most of the recipes in this cookbook are relatively quick to prepare. For simplicity's sake, I hadn't intended for any to use yeast. But since there's nothing like donuts on Halloween (or at breakfast time, play group, ...), I couldn't resist including this donut recipe (and then a few more yeasted recipes after that)! Making yeasted donuts can be a great rainy day indoor family activity. Perhaps as your children are watching the dough rise, you can even get in a quick science lesson.

Extra tools needed:
One extra bowl in which dough can rise
Two light dish towels for covering rising dough
One small pot for heating wet ingredients
One baking thermometer
One large cookie tray
One rolling pin
One 2 ¼ inch donut cutter (If you don't have one, use 2 round cookie cutters, each a different size, or, if that is not possible, use the top of a floured drinking cup for the outer circle, and then cut out a middle circle the size of a quarter with the tip of a spoon.)
Plastic wrap
One large, heavy, deep pan or skillet
Plates covered with lots of paper towels for soaking up oil from donuts
Slotted spoon or spatula for lowering donuts into and raising them out of oil
Paper (or plastic) bag for shaking donut in powdered sugar

Pan Ingredients:
Approximately 3 quarts of high temperature cooking oil (Note, if you don't want to use so much oil, try using a small pot and just

cooking 1 or 2 donuts at a time, checking from time to time to make sure the oil has remained sufficiently hot.)

Dry Ingredients:
1 ¼ c white spelt flour
½ c sugar
1/3 c potato starch
2 Tbsp arrowroot flour
2 ¼ tsp dry yeast
1 tsp tapioca starch
3/4 tsp cinnamon
1/8 tsp cloves
1/8 tsp ginger
1/8 tsp nutmeg

Wet Ingredients:
½ c rice milk
1/3 c apple juice (or apple cider)
2 Tbsp canola or safflower oil
1 Tbsp water
½ tsp vanilla

Additional Ingredients:
Approximately 1 c white spelt flour
¼ tsp salt
1 - 2 tsp safflower oil

Optional ingredient:
Powdered sugar

Mix dry ingredients well with fork, and set aside until at room temperature.

Put wet ingredients into a small pot. Stirring occasionally, heat to approximately 125°F. (120°F – 130°F is ok. If it gets too hot, let sit to cool to 125°F. If you want to help it cool quickly back down to 125°F, pour it out of the hot pot into a different pot or bowl.)

Add wet ingredients to dry ingredients.

Using an electric mixer, mix on medium speed for 4 minutes. The batter will be bubbling during the mixing, and by the end will be very stretchy and sticky. Add about 1/8 cup (2 Tbsp) of the "additional" flour and mix until it is also absorbed. Turn off mixer, scraping off as much dough as possible off the beaters into the bowl.

Add about 1/3 of a cup of flour, and stir in with spatula. If still extremely sticky, add a couple more tablespoons of flour.

Mix about 1 Tbsp of flour with the salt and spread mixture over a cutting board or smooth table.

Knead the dough on that surface for about 6 minutes. (To knead dough: Put one hand over the other, with both palms down, and then push down and a little bit forward on the dough a few times with the ball of your bottom hand, using the weight of your body. Then, without tearing the dough, fold the dough over towards you to make it thick again. Keep repeating the process, turning the dough in different directions from time to time.) Any time a spot is sticky, spread a teaspoon or two of the "additional" flour over the sticky area, using no more than necessary. You may need a bit more or less than the 1 cup. When through, the dough should be soft and springy and no longer very sticky. End with the dough in a slightly flattened ball shape.

Place the "additional ingredient" oil, into a mixing bowl, oiling the bowl, and leaving the remaining oil in the bottom of the bowl. Place the dough ball in the bowl, and roll it around until the dough is greased. Cover the bowl with a damp dish towel, and put the bowl in a warm (80°F to 85°F if possible), non-drafty place for 40 minutes. (One way to achieve something close to this is to turn on the oven, turn it off when it reaches 100°F, and put it in there, leaving the oven off.)

While the dough is rising, clean any stuck dough off the kneading area, and then lightly flour it again so that it is ready for later. Also lightly flour the cookie tray.

When the dough is ready, you ought to be able to leave a deep impression if you stick a couple of fingers deep into the dough. Otherwise, leave for a few more minutes.

In the bowl, punch down dough (about 20 punches) to get rid of any air. Break the dough into two pieces (or three if your work area is small). Place the first piece of dough on the prepared kneading area. Roll the dough to between 1/3 and ½ inch thick. Cut with the donut cutter. Carefully remove the inner circle from each donut, and place (trying not to stretch it) the donut onto a floured cookie sheet. If you would like to cook the donut "holes", put them on the tray as well. Otherwise, consider them scraps. Gather all scraps, form a ball with them, roll it, and repeat the processes until all the dough has been used.

Cover donuts with plastic wrap, and then with dish towel over that. Again place in warm non-drafty location and let rise for about an hour – a finger pushing on a donut should leave an indentation.

Heat, on low, a large, heavy pan/skillet. Pour in enough oil to fill pan about one inch deep (oil should come less than half way up the side of the pan). Increase temperature gradually. If you have a cooking thermometer, try to maintain the oil temperature at about 375°F. The goal is to have the pan hot enough that the donuts don't soak up too much of the oil, but not so hot that the oil will brown or smoke. Depending on your oil, the range may be approximately 350°F – 400°F.

One at a time, pausing for about half a minute after each donut, use spatula to lower donuts into hot oil. This slow rotation will allow pan to stay at a stable (hot) temperature. If crumbs start to build up in pan, clean them out before adding more donuts. At any one time, maintain no more than 3 or 4 donuts in the pan (or 1 or 2 if using a very small pot).

Cook each donut 1 to 1 ½ minutes on each side, so that it is nicely browned.

Remove with metal spatula, allowing donut to drip into pan briefly before setting it on paper towels.

Change paper towels as needed, so that there is dry area available to soak up excess oil from donuts.

Eat as is. Or if desired, put powdered sugar and donuts (a few at a time) into a bag, seal, and shake gently.

French Toast

Bread Ingredients:
4 – 6 slices raisin (or regular) very tasty bread. (Number will vary with size, thickness, and absorbency of the bread.)

Bowl Ingredients:
½ c rice milk   1 tsp vanilla extract
2 Tbsp maple syrup   ½ tsp salt
1 tsp cinnamon

Additional Ingredients:
1 Tbsp apple juice   1 Tbsp tapioca starch
Canola (or other oil) for generously oiling the pan

Heat bread in a toaster oven on 300°F briefly if fresh, or for 2-5 minutes if frozen, until a bit dry but not browned or crunchy.

Put "bowl ingredients" into a mixing bowl. Stir with fork.

Put tapioca starch in a small dish. Add apple juice and stir until the texture is smooth. Add mixture to the rest of the ingredients.

Beat with an electric mixer for about 15 seconds on low, then about a minute on high. If the bottom of the bowl is very rounded, pour batter into a flat bowl; otherwise, leave in mixing bowl.

For each piece of bread: Set the piece of bread in the batter for a couple of seconds and then flip it to barely coat the other side and remove. The trick here is not to let the bread get soggy.

Heat skillet on medium heat, add oil and heat. Add bread to fit. After a minute, cover for a minute (for very thin slices) or two (for thicker slices). Then uncover for the rest of cooking. Turn when browned, adding more oil if needed. Remove from pan when the other side is also browned. Repeat with remaining slices. Serve immediately, or refrigerate or freeze to reheat another day.

Most people like maple syrup on French Toast, but you might also experiment with apple sauce, apple butter, Cherry (or other fruit) Syrup (see p. 123), strawberry sauce (see p. 124), or fruit.

Granola

Pre-heat oven to 250°F.
Large broiler pan (approximately 15" x 13" x 1")

Ingredients:
1 c rice bran
½ c white rice flour
½ c brown rice flour
1 c sesame seeds, raw, unhulled (optional. Note: some people with nut allergies are also allergic to sesame seeds)
¾ c sunflower seeds, raw, unsalted (optional, if allergies permit)
1 Tbsp cinnamon
5 c rolled oats (not instant)
¾ c canola oil
¾ c maple syrup
1 c dried raisins or other dried fruit*

In a very large bowl or pot, mix together all ingredients except the oats, oil, syrup, and fruit. Add oats and mix again. In separate bowl (or in the measuring cup!) mix the oil with the syrup. Pour into the dry ingredients and mix until well blended. Spread mixture onto the bottom of the pan. Using a large spoon or spatula, pat down the mixture until it is flat, especially pressing down if you like chunks in your granola.

Bake for 25 minutes and then turn over the granola with a large spatula. Bake for 20 minutes more. Remove from oven, add the dried fruit, and mix gently. (The "gently" is again assuming you would like to keep chunks.) Let cool in pan.

*Other fruit options: Try a mix of ½ c chopped dates rolled in oat flour with ½ c raisins. Or try freeze-dried berries, dried cranberries or chopped dried apricots. (Note: Dried apricots get their bright color from metabisulphites, a common allergen. If this is a concern, use organic dried apricots, which will have an almost brown color.)

Cranberry Granola

Dry Ingredients:
1 c oat flour
1 c oat bran
½ c light brown sugar

2/3 c sugar
2 Tbsp tapioca starch
1 tsp salt

Additional Dry Ingredient:
4 c oat flakes (old fashioned)

Wet Ingredients:
¼ c canola (or safflower) oil
¼ c orange juice

3 Tbsp maple syrup (grade B)
1 Tbsp molasses

Additional Ingredients:
¾ c fresh cranberries if using the granola within a couple of days; otherwise, ¾ c dried or frozen cranberries (or other berries)

Pre-heat oven to 275°F.

Loosen packed brown sugar. In a large bowl or pot, mix together dry ingredients thoroughly with fork. Add the oats and stir again.

Put wet ingredients into a bowl or measuring cup, and mix.

Pour wet into dry, and fold two or three times. If using fresh cranberries, add them now. (Dried fruit will be added later.) Continue to fold until just mixed.

Spread mixture onto the bottom of a large ungreased broiler pan (approximately 15" x 13" x 1"). Using a large spoon or spatula, press down the mixture until it is flat and compressed. (Or, for fun with kids: Loosely cover dough in pan with plastic wrap. Over the wrap, roll the batter with a rolling pin or a flat glass. Then use hands to further compress, especially around edges. Remove the wrap.)

Bake for 25 minutes and then turn over the granola with a spatula, pressing it firmly again. Bake for 20 minutes more. Remove from oven, add the dried fruit (if not using fresh), and mix gently. (The "gently" is assuming you would like to keep a few chunks.)

Quick Pancakes
(makes about 10 4" pancakes)

Dry Ingredients:

¾ c whole spelt flour   1 ¼ tsp baking powder
¾ c white spelt flour   1 Tbsp tapioca starch
 1 tsp soy lecithin powder   ¼ tsp salt

Wet Ingredients:

2/3 c rice milk   2 Tbsp apple sauce
1/3 c safflower oil   2 Tbsp maple syrup
½ c water (room temperature)   ½ tsp vanilla extract
2 Tbsp additional water

Wet Ingredients:

Canola (or other) oil for cooking

Put dry ingredients into a bowl and stir well with a fork.

Measure wet ingredients directly into a 2 cup measuring cup. (If you measure the ingredients in the order listed, it will be easy to use the cup's measuring lines.) Beat briefly with a fork.

Pour wet into dry, and mix with the fork until flour is almost all blended. The pancakes will be best with minimal stirring, so it is alright to leave an occasional small spot of flour.

Heat skillet on medium/low. Add oil. When the oil is hot enough that a drop of batter dropped in it sizzles, pour in batter of the size desired. Tilt pan if needed to spread batter. Cover the pan loosely until the edges (outer ½ inch or so) of the pancakes are cooked and the batter in the middle is bubbling. (It is fine to uncover the pan periodically to check on progress and to adjust temperature if needed to prevent burning.) Then flip with a firm spatula, and cook uncovered until new bottom is lightly browned. For each new pancake, add a bit of oil to the pan. (Hint: Try spreading the oil by scraping it with the spatula over the bottom of the pan.) For fun, you might try making a giant pancake, the whole size of the pan!

Quick Blueberry Pancakes

Follow recipe for Quick Pancakes (see page 29). After pouring wet into dry, mix with fork until flour is almost blended. Add ½ c blueberries, and stir until flour is mostly blended. Cook as instructed.

Quick Waffles
(makes 5-6 waffles)

Follow recipe for Quick Pancakes (see page 29), but reduce the ½ c water to 1/3 c. Cook according to instructions of waffle maker.

Try drizzled with Cherry (or other fruit) Syrup (see page 123).

Quick Blueberry Waffles
(makes 5-6 waffles)

Follow recipe for Quick Pancakes (see page 29), but reduce the ½ c water to 1/3 c. After pouring wet into dry, mix until flour is about three quarters blended. Add ½ c blueberries, and stir until flour is almost all blended. Cook according to instructions of your waffle maker.

Muffins, Quick Breads, and Tea Cakes

Apple Muffins
(makes 12 sweet, light, full-sized muffins)

Pre-heat oven to 350°F. Oil muffin tin.

Dry Ingredients:
1 1/3 c white spelt flour
1 c whole spelt flour
2/3 c sugar
½ c + 4 tsp potato starch
½ tsp xanthan gum

2 tsp lecithin powder
2 tsp baking powder
1 tsp baking soda
4 tsp cinnamon
½ tsp salt

Wet Ingredients:
2/3 c safflower oil
½ c apple juice
½ c applesauce

¼ c water
¼ c maple syrup
1 tsp vanilla extract

Extra Ingredients:
1 1/3 c chopped apples
Cinnamon sugar (Mix 2 tsp sugar with 1 tsp cinnamon) - optional

Mix dry ingredients together and sift 3 times.

Put wet ingredients into blender, and blend on low for 15 seconds and then on high for 1 minute.

Pour wet into dry, and fold gently until almost mixed. Then add apples and fold until barely mixed.

Spoon into muffin tin.

Optional: Sprinkle lightly with cinnamon sugar.

Cook 35 – 40 minutes, until springs to the touch.

Let cool in pan on cooling rack for 5 minutes, and remove from pan and cool on cooling rack.

Apple Oat Cereal Muffins

I said to my friend, "I'm making oatmeal. Will your kids eat that?" She responded, "I wish!" With some of the leftover oatmeal, I created this recipe. With the resulting muffins, her wish came true!

Pre-heat oven to 350°F. Oil muffin tin.

Dry Ingredients:

1 1/3 c white spelt flour   1 tsp xanthan gum
1 c whole spelt flour   1 tsp salt
1/2 c + 4 tsp potato starch   1 tsp baking soda
2 Tbsp cinnamon   1 ½ tsp baking powder
1 ½ tsp soy lecithin powder

Wet Ingredients:

½ c rice milk   1/3 c safflower oil
½ c maple syrup   1/3 c brown sugar
½ c applesauce   1 tsp lemon juice
2/3 c leftover oatmeal (Preferably, use non-instant oatmeal cooked just in water until soft and thick, and then refrigerated long enough to firm up quite solid.)

Additional Ingredients:

1 ½ c peeled, chopped apples (almost 2 apples)

Mix dry ingredients together thoroughly. Sift 3 times. Set aside.
Put wet ingredients in blender. Blend on low for 15 seconds and then high for 1 minute.
Pour wet into dry, and fold gently until almost mixed. Add chopped apple and fold gently until just mixed.
Spoon into muffin tin. The batter will go above top of pan.
Cook 40 minutes, or until muffins spring to the touch and a toothpick comes out clean.

Apple Rice Cereal Muffins
(makes one dozen muffins)

Pre-heat oven to 350°F. Oil muffin tin.

Dry Ingredients:

1 ½ c white rice flour

½ c sorghum flour

¾ c potato starch

2 Tbsp cinnamon

4 tsp tapioca starch

1 tsp xanthan gum

1 tsp salt

1 ½ tsp baking soda

1 ½ tsp baking powder

1 ½ tsp soy lecithin powder

Wet Ingredients:

½ c rice milk

½ c safflower oil

2 Tbsp water

½ c light brown sugar

2/3 c applesauce

½ c maple syrup

1 Tbsp lemon juice

1/3 c leftover cream of rice cereal (Preferably, cooked just in water until soft and thick, and then refrigerated to thicken more, then again brought to room temperature)

Additional Ingredients:

1 ¾ c peeled, chopped apples (almost 2 apples)

Optional Ingredients:

A spoonful of light brown sugar to sprinkle on top of muffins

Mix dry ingredients together thoroughly. Sift 3 times. Set aside.

Put wet ingredients in blender. Blend on low for a few seconds and then on high speed for about a minute.

Pour wet into dry, and fold gently until almost mixed. Add chopped apple and fold gently until just mixed.

Spoon into muffin tin. The batter will go above top of the tin. (Don't worry – these don't grow much in the oven, so they shouldn't spill over!) Cook 35 - 40 minutes, or until muffins spring to the touch and a toothpick comes out clean.

Blueberry Muffins
(makes one dozen smallish muffins)

Pre-heat oven to 350°F. Oil 1 muffin tin.

Dry Ingredients:

1 ¼ c white spelt flour*
¼ c whole spelt flour*
¾ c sugar
¼ c potato starch
1 Tbsp potato starch

1 tsp soy lecithin powder
1 tsp baking powder
½ tsp baking soda
½ tsp xanthan gum
¼ tsp salt

Wet Ingredients:

1/3 c pear juice
2 Tbsp lemon juice

1/3 c safflower oil
1/3 c ripe (or canned) sliced
Bartlett pear (about ½ pear)

Extra Ingredients:

1 ¼ c fresh or frozen blueberries

Mix dry ingredients together, and sift 3 times.

Put wet ingredients in blender.

If using frozen berries, thaw by rinsing with cold water in colander or strainer. Pat dry, sprinkle with the tsp of flour, and stir to coat the berries. If using fresh berries, wash and dry only.

Blend wet ingredients on low for about 15 seconds, then on high for about a minute.

Pour wet into dry and fold gently until almost blended. Add blueberries and fold until just blended. Spoon into muffin tin.

Cook for 35 minutes, or until springs to the touch, and toothpick comes out clean. Cool in tin for 5 minutes, then on cooling rack.

*Optional: The spelt flours can be substituted with 1 c barley flour and ½ c oat flour.

Carrot Spice Muffins and Bread
(makes one dozen muffins and one small loaf.)

This is one of my favorites for bringing to restaurants (a slice) and packing lunch boxes (a muffin). So, this recipe makes both!

Oil muffin tin and small loaf pan (3 ½" x 7 ½").

Dry Ingredients:

1 ¼ c white rice flour
1 ¼ c sugar
2/3 c + 4 tsp potato starch
½ c sorghum flour
2 tsp cinnamon
1 ½ tsp soy lecithin powder
1 tsp baking soda

1 tsp baking powder
1 tsp xanthan gum
1 tsp salt
1 tsp ground ginger
½ tsp cloves
¼ tsp nutmeg

Wet Ingredients:

¾ c safflower oil
½ c rice milk
2/3 c banana (about 1 ½ medium bananas)

1 Tbsp water
1 Tbsp lemon juice
½ c applesauce

Additional Ingredients:

1 c tightly packed finely chopped in food processor (or grated) carrots (3-4 carrots)
½ c raisins (optional)

Mix dry ingredients, sift 3 times, and set aside.
Put wet ingredients in blender and let warm to room temperature.
Pre-heat oven to 350°F.
Blend wet ingredients on low for 15 seconds and on high for 60.
Pour wet into dry, and fold gently until almost mixed. Add carrot, and if desired, raisins, and fold gently until just mixed.
Spoon batter just above top of muffin tin, and remaining batter into loaf pan. Cook 38-40 minutes, or until springs to the touch.

Chocolate Chip Banana Rice Muffins
(Makes one dozen small, sweet brown muffins,
nice for a gluten-free treat right out of the oven)

Dry Ingredients:
1/2 c white rice flour
1/3 c sorghum flour
¼ c potato starch
2/3 c sugar
1 tsp cinnamon

1 tsp soy lecithin powder
1 tsp baking soda
½ tsp baking powder
½ tsp xanthan gum
½ tsp salt

Wet Ingredients:
2 Tbsp safflower oil
2 Tbsp maple syrup
2 Tbsp apple sauce

2 Tbsp rice milk
1 Tbsp lemon juice

¾ c (tightly packed) ripe banana (about 2 small bananas)

Additional Ingredients:
1/3 c chocolate chips

Put dry ingredients in large mixing bowl and mix with fork. Sift
3 times and set aside.Put wet ingredients in blender, and let sit until
room temperature.

Preheat oven to 350°F. Oil a muffin pan.

Blend wet ingredients on low for about 15 seconds, then on high
speed for about a minute.

Pour wet into dry, and fold gently until almost mixed. Add
chocolate chips, and fold them in gently.

Fill each muffin cup about ¾ full. They will not overflow, since
these muffins do not rise. Bake for 30 minutes. Let cool in pan on
a rack for 5 minutes. Then dump out onto cooling rack and cool
(that is, unless they get eaten first – these are delicious warm, full of
melted chocolate.)

Let cool in pan on a cooling rack.

Cranberry Muffins
(makes one dozen full, delicious muffins)

Dry Ingredients:
¾ c white spelt flour

2/3 c whole spelt flour

2/3 c sugar

2 Tbsp potato starch

1 Tbsp tapioca starch

1 tsp lecithin powder

2 tsp cinnamon

1 tsp baking powder

½ tsp baking soda

½ tsp xanthan gum

¼ tsp salt

Wet Ingredients:
1/3 c applesauce

1/3 c orange juice

¼ c light brown sugar, tightly packed

1/3 c safflower oil

2 Tbsp rice milk

Additional Ingredients:
¾ c fresh cranberries

½ c rolled oats (non-instant)

2 tsp sugar

Lightly oil 1 muffin pan.

Wash cranberries, tossing and replacing any that aren't firm. Pat dry with paper towels and then air dry.

Mix dry ingredients, sift 3 times, and set aside.

Put wet ingredients in blender and let sit until room temperature. When almost room temperature, preheat oven to 350°F.

Blend wet ingredients on low for 15 seconds and on high for 60.

Pour wet into dry. Fold gently only until there are no very wet sections, and much but not all of the flour is incorporated. Add oats and cranberries gradually - about ¼ of them at a time – while continuing to fold gently until just mixed.

Fill each tin section with a heaping spoonful of dough.

Sprinkle tops with the sugar. Cook 30 minutes, or until springs to the touch and toothpick (not hitting cranberries!) comes out clean.

Cool in pan on cooling rack, but loosen in pan after 5 minutes.

Peach Muffins
(makes 1 dozen large, light, mildly sweetened muffins)

Dry Ingredients:

1 1/3 c white spelt flour

1 c whole spelt flour

½ c potato starch

½ c sugar

1 Tbsp cinnamon

1 Tbsp tapioca starch

1 ½ tsp baking powder

1 tsp lecithin powder

1 tsp baking soda

1 tsp xanthan gum

½ tsp salt

½ tsp cloves

½ tsp powdered ginger

¼ tsp nutmeg

Wet Ingredients:

2/3 c safflower oil

1 c peach nectar (or apple juice)

½ c chopped peaches (fresh, canned, or frozen)

¼ c maple syrup

1 tsp vanilla extract

Extra Ingredients:

2 c chopped fresh or frozen peaches

2 Tbsp sugar

1 Tbsp white spelt flour

2 tsp cinnamon

2 tsp sugar (optional)

Mix dry ingredients and sift 3 times.

Put wet ingredients in blender and set aside.

If using frozen peaches, rinse if frosty, pat dry, and let thaw.

Pre-heat oven to 350°F. Oil muffin tin.

Mix the extra ingredient spelt flour, 2 Tbsp sugar, and cinnamon. Toss the peaches in the cinnamon mixture to coat the peaches.

Blend wet ingredients for 15 seconds on low and 60 on high.

Pour wet into dry, and fold gently until almost mixed. Add the peach mixture and fold until barely mixed .

Spoon into muffin tin filling to above top of pan.

For added sweetness, sprinkle tops with sugar if desired.

Cook for 35 minutes, until springs to the touch. Set pan on cooling rack for 5 minutes. Then cool directly on rack.

Pumpkin Muffins
(makes 12 small muffins)

Pre-heat oven to 350°F. Oil muffin pan.

Dry Ingredients:

1 c barley flour*
½ c oat flour*
3/4 c sugar
¼ c potato starch
2 tsp cinnamon
1 tsp soy lecithin powder
1 tsp xanthan gum

½ tsp baking soda
½ tsp baking powder
¼ tsp salt
¼ tsp ginger
¼ tsp cloves
¼ tsp nutmeg

Wet Ingredients:

2/3 c canned pumpkin
½ c rice milk
½ c apple juice

1/3 c safflower oil
1 tsp vanilla extract

Optional Ingredients:

1/3 c raisins

Mix dry ingredients, and sift 3 times.

Put wet ingredients in blender. Blend for 15 seconds on low and one minute on high.

Pour wet into dry, and fold gently until almost mixed. Add raisins if using, and fold until just mixed.

Pour into muffin tin. Cook 40 minutes or until springs to the touch, and a toothpick comes out clean.

Set pan on cooling rack for 1-2 minutes. Remove muffins from pan and cool on cooling rack.

* For gluten free alternative, replace barley and oat flour with: 3/4 c buckwheat flour, 1/3 c amaranth flour, and 1/8 c rice bran, and increase potato starch to 1/3 c. Add 2 tsp sugar, and a pinch more of each spice. You may need to bake 1-2 minutes longer.

Banana Bread
(makes two loaves)

Pre-heat oven to 350°F. Oil two 8 ½" x 4 ½" bread pans.

Dry Ingredients:

1 ½ c white spelt flour*	1 tsp baking soda
1 c whole spelt flour*	1 tsp baking powder
1 ¼ c sugar	1 tsp xanthan gum
½ c potato starch	1 Tbsp cinnamon
4 tsp tapioca starch	½ tsp salt
2 tsp soy lecithin powder	

Wet Ingredients:

2/3 c rice milk*	1 Tbsp lemon juice
½ c safflower oil	1 tsp vanilla extract

1 ½ c tightly packed ripe banana (about 3-4 bananas!)*

Additional Ingredients:

½ c chopped flour-dusted dates (Hint: Chop on heavily floured cutting board for easy, non-sticky chopping and flouring.)

Optional Ingredients:

Substitute some or all of the dates with chocolate chips or large raisins

Mix dry ingredients, and sift 3 times.

Put wet ingredients in blender. Blend for 15 seconds on low and one minute on high.

Pour wet into dry, and fold gently until almost mixed. Add dates (raisins/chocolate chips), and fold until just mixed.

Pour into bread pans. Cook 50 minutes or until springs to the touch, and a toothpick comes out clean. Let cool in pans on cooling rack.

* Or replace spelt flours with 1 ½ c barley flour and 1 c oat flour; use 3/4 cup rice milk and 1 ¼ c banana. Bake for 51 minutes.

Banana Rice Bread
(makes two loaves)

Dry Ingredients:
1 1/8 c (1 c plus 2 Tbsp) sugar
1 c white rice flour
2/3 c sorghum flour
1/3 c potato starch
1 Tbsp tapioca starch
1 Tbsp cinnamon

2 tsp soy lecithin powder
1 tsp xanthan gum
1 tsp baking soda
1 tsp baking powder
½ tsp salt

Wet Ingredients:
1/3 c safflower oil
2 Tbsp honey
¼ c apple sauce

2 Tbsp apple juice
2 Tbsp lemon juice
1 ½ c (tightly packed) banana
(about 3 bananas)

Additional Ingredients:
¼ c (tightly packed) chopped pitted dates (about 6 small or 3 large dates) rolled in rice (or other) flour (Hint: Chop on heavily floured cutting board for easy, non-sticky chopping and flouring.)
½ c raisins (optional)

Mix dry ingredients and sift 3 times. Set aside.

Put wet ingredients in blender, and let sit to warm to room temperature.

Preheat oven to 350°F. Oil two 8 ½" x 4 ½" loaf pans.

Blend wet ingredients on low speed for 15 seconds, then on high speed for a minute.

Pour wet into dry, and fold gently until almost mixed. Add dates, and if using raisins or chocolate chips, add them as well. Fold them in gently.

Pour into baking pans. Bake for 1 hour or until toothpick comes out clean. Let cool in pan on a cooling rack.

Corn Bread

(Darker in color than traditional corn bread, due to the color of the sorghum flour. Best when fresh out of the oven.)

Pre-heat oven to 350°F. Oil one 4 ½ x 8 ½ bread pan.

Dry Ingredients:

1/3 c sorghum flour

2/3 c corn flour (Hint: If your flour has some coarse grains that you would prefer not be in your bread, measure the 2/3 cup. Sift the corn flour by itself, allowing the coarse grains to get caught in the sifter. Measure the caught grain before throwing it away. Add that much new corn flour to replenish the 2/3 cup.)

¼ c potato starch

2 Tbsp sugar

1 ½ tsp tapioca starch

1 tsp soy lecithin powder

1 tsp baking powder

½ tsp baking soda

½ tsp salt

½ tsp xanthan gum

Wet Ingredients:

½ c fresh (or canned) Bartlett pear, peeled, sliced, and firmly packed

½ c safflower oil

¼ c applesauce

¼ c maple syrup

1 Tbsp rice milk

    Mix dry ingredients together with a fork, then sift 3 times.

    Put wet ingredients into blender. Blend on low speed for 15 seconds and then on high speed for 1 minute.

    Pour wet into dry, and fold gently until just mixed.

    Pour into bread pan. Cook 40 minutes until springs to the touch, and a toothpick comes out clean.

[Co, So, GF, LNS]

Zucchini Carrot Corn Bread
(very moist; best when fresh out of the oven)

Pre-heat oven to 350°F. Oil two 4 ½ x 8 ½ bread pans.

Dry Ingredients:

1 1/3 c corn flour

2/3 c sorghum flour

½ c + 1 Tbsp potato starch

¼ c sugar

1 ½ tsp baking powder

1 tsp baking soda

1 tsp salt

1 tsp xanthan gum

1 tsp soy lecithin powder

Wet Ingredients:

2/3 c safflower oil

½ c applesauce

½ c maple syrup

2 Tbsp rice milk

1 c fresh (or canned) sliced Bartlett pear (about 1 pear)

(the zucchini/carrot juice prepared below)

Prepare zucchini and carrot:

Grate one small zucchini and one carrot (on 2nd to largest shredding size on grater). Let shredded pieces sit in a bowl for at least 20 minutes. Then squeeze out the juices (about 2 Tbsp) and put juices into blender. Measure 1 ¼ cups zucchini (loosely packed) and 2/3 cup carrot, and set this aside for the end of the recipe. (Hint: If there is any leftover zucchini or carrot, try throwing it into spaghetti sauce, hamburger meat, mashed potatos, or at the end of a stir fry.)

Sift the corn flour. If some coarse grains get caught in the sifter, you may choose to toss them and replace them with more flour. This will yield a slightly lighter bread than if you leave the grains in.

Mix dry ingredients and sift 3 times.

Put wet ingredients in blender. Blend on low for 15 seconds and on high for 1 minute.

Pour wet into dry, and fold gently until almost mixed. Loosen vegetable mixture if tightly packed, and then add it to the batter.

Pour into bread pans. Cook 40 - 45 minutes until springs to the touch, and a toothpick comes out clean.

Cranberry Bread
(makes 2 loaves)

Preheat oven to 350°F. Lightly oil 2 loaf pans.

Dry Ingredients:

1 c + 2 Tbsp white spelt flour
1 c whole spelt flour
¼ c potato starch
1 c + 2 Tbsp sugar
4 ½ tsp tapioca starch
1 Tbsp cinnamon

1 ½ tsp baking powder
1 ½ tsp lecithin powder
1 tsp xanthan gum
½ tsp baking soda
½ tsp salt

Wet Ingredients:

½ c safflower oil
½ c light brown sugar, tightly packed
½ c applesauce

½ c orange juice *
¼ c rice milk *

Additional Ingredients:

¾ c rolled oats (non-instant, loosely packed)
1 ½ c fresh cranberries
2 tsp sugar

Wash cranberries, replacing any that are not firm Pat and air dry.
Mix dry ingredients, sift 3 times, and set aside.
Put wet ingredients in blender, and let sit until room temperature.
Blend wet ingredients on low for 15 seconds and on high for 60.
Pour wet into dry. Fold a few times. Add oats and cranberries
gradually while continuing to fold until just mixed. Spoon into pans.
Sprinkle tops with the 2 tsp sugar. Cook 55 minutes, or until
spring to the touch . Cool in pans on rack, loosening after 5 minutes.

* **Optional:** For a stronger orange flavor, use 1 - 2 additional Tbsp
of orange juice in place of the same amount of rice milk.

Peach Bread
(a lightly sweetened bread)

Pre-heat oven to 350°F. Oil two 8 ½" by 4 ½" loaf pans.

Dry Ingredients:
1 1/3 c barley flour (or whole spelt flour)
1 c oat flour (or white spelt flour)
2/3 c sugar
½ c potato starch
2 tsp cinnamon
1 tsp soy lecithin powder
1 tsp baking soda

1 tsp xanthan gum
1 tsp baking powder
½ tsp salt
¼ tsp ginger
¼ (or 1/8) tsp cloves
1/8 tsp nutmeg

Wet Ingredients:
¾ c peach nectar (or mango or apple)
¼ c maple syrup
1/3 c sliced peaches (fresh, canned or frozen)

½ c safflower oil
1 tsp vanilla extract

Extra Ingredients:
1 ¼ c chopped fresh (or thawed frozen) peaches
1 Tbsp barley (or white spelt) flour
1 Tbsp sugar.
1 more Tbsp sugar

Mix dry ingredients and sift 3 times.

Put wet ingredients in blender. Blend on low for 15 seconds and on high for 1 minute.

Mix Barley (or spelt) flour with one of the Tbsp's of sugar. Sprinkle it over peaches and mix briefly.

Pour wet into dry, and fold gently until almost mixed. Add fruit mixture and fold until just mixed.

Spoon into loaf pans, and sprinkle tops with the final sugar.

Bake for 50 minutes, until springs to the touch, and a toothpick comes out clean.

Nectarine Bread, Mango Bread, and Apple Bread

Follow the recipe for Peach Bread (p. 46).

For **Nectarine Bread**, substitute nectarines for the peaches. Increase sugar to 3/4 c.

For **Mango Bread,** substitute mangos for the peaches. Use mango nectar for the juice if possible. Otherwise, use peach nectar, peach juice, or apple juice.

For **Apple Bread,** substitute apples for the peaches. Remove the ginger, cloves, and nutmeg, and increase the cinnamon to 1 Tbsp. Use apple juice, and replace the wet ingredient 1/3 c fruit with ¼ c apple sauce.

Wholesome Zucchini Carrot Date Bread

Pre-heat oven to 350°F. Oil two 4 ½ x 8 ½ bread pans.

Dry Ingredients:
1 c white spelt flour
1 ¾ c whole spelt flour
½ c potato starch
1/3 c quinoi flour
2 Tbsp rice bran
4 ½ tsp tapioca starch
2 tsp soy lecithin powder

1 tsp xanthan gum
1 tsp baking powder
1 tsp baking soda
½ tsp salt
4 tsp cinnamon
¼ tsp nutmeg
¼ tsp cloves

Wet Ingredients:
½ c safflower oil
½ c rice milk
½ c ripe banana (about 1 banana)
½ c maple syrup (preferably grade B)
(the zucchini/carrot juice prepared below)

½ c applesauce
1/4 c apple juice
1 tsp vanilla extract
1 tsp lemon juice

Other Ingredients:
1 ¼ c grated zuccini, tightly packed (about one small/medium zucchini, grated on 2nd to largest shredding size on grater)
¼ c similarly grated carrot, tightly packed (about one small carrot)
1/3 c pitted, chopped dates, tightly packed (about 9)
1 – 3 tsp whole spelt flour (as needed depending dates' wetness)

Let shredded vegetables sit for at least 20 minutes. Squeeze out 2 Tbsp of juices (yes, I do this with my hands) and add to blender , supplementing with water if needed. Loosen vegetables with a fork.

Mix dry ingredients, sift 3 times, and set aside.

Toss the dates in the 1-3 tsp flour until completely coated.

Pour wet ingredients into dry, and fold gently until almost mixed. Add the vegetables and dates. Fold until barely blended. Pour into pans. Cook 55 minutes or until springs to the touch.

Zucchini Bread

Oil two 4 ½ x 8 ½ bread pans.

Dry Ingredients:

1 1/3 c whole spelt flour
1 1/4 c white spelt flour
½ c potato starch
½ c sugar
4 tsp tapioca starch
3 ½ tsp cinnamon
1 tsp soy lecithin powder

1 tsp baking powder
1 tsp baking soda
1 tsp xanthan gum
½ tsp salt
¼ tsp nutmeg
¼ tsp cloves

Wet Ingredients:

½ c safflower oil
½ c rice milk
½ c applesauce
1/3 c ripe banana
¼ c tightly packed chopped dates (about 6)
(the zucchini juice prepared below)

1/3 c water
3 tbsp maple syrup
1 tsp vanilla extract
¼ tsp lemon juice

Additional Ingredients:

1 c grated zuccini, tightly packed
½ c raisins or ¼ c chocolate chips (optional)

Let shredded vegetables sit for at least 20 minutes while putting wet ingredients in blender. Squeeze out 2 Tbsp of juices (yes, I do this with my hands) and add to blender , supplementing with water if needed. Toss the zucchini with a fork to loosen, and set aside.

Mix dry ingredients and sift 3 times.

Put wet ingredients into blender to sit until room temperature. Then pre-heat oven to 350°F, and blend wet ingredients on low for 15 seconds and then on high for 1 minute.

Pour wet into dry, and fold gently until partially mixed. Then add the zucchini gradually while gently folding until just mixed.

Pour into pans. Cook 55-57 minutes or until springs to the touch.

Tea Hee Hee Cake
(This wholesome, subtly flavored cake is nice with tea.
It is very lightly sweetened.)

Pre-heat oven to 350°F. Oil one 9" x 12" cake pan.

Dry Ingredients:

1 ½ c whole spelt flour

1 ¼ c white spelt flour

½ c + 4 tsp potato starch

¼ c rice bran

2 Tbsp date (or turbinado or white) sugar

1 Tbsp cinnamon

2 tsp lecithin powder

1 ½ tsp baking powder

1 tsp baking soda

½ tsp xanthan gum

½ tsp salt

½ tsp cardamon

Wet Ingredients:

½ c safflower oil

½ c rice milk

½ c maple syrup

1 tsp lime (or lemon) juice

2 chopped dates (preferably not very soft)

2/3 c banana, tightly packed (about 1 ½ medium bananas)

1/3 c water

¼ c apple sauce

1 tsp vanilla extract

Extra Ingredient:

¾ c raisins

Mix dry ingredients, sift 3 times, and set aside.

Put wet ingredients in blender. Blend on low for 15 seconds and on high for 1 minute.

Pour wet into dry, and fold gently until almost mixed. Add raisins and fold until just mixed.

Spoon into cake pan.

Cook for 40 minutes until springs to the touch and a toothpick comes out clean.

Cool in pan, on cooling rack.

Serve warm or at room temperature.

Snack Bars and Brownies

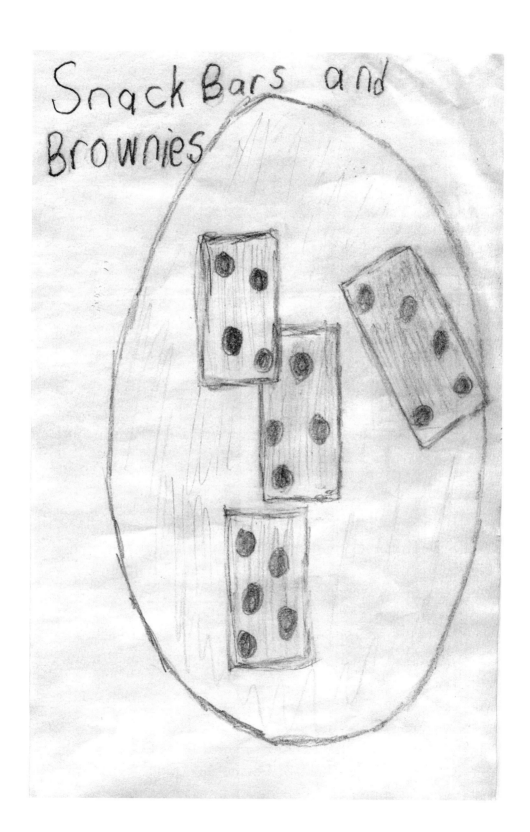

Apricot Oat Bars
(a slightly lemony bar with a brownie-like consistency)

Dry Ingredients:
½ c oat flour
½ c barley flour
1/3 c sugar
1 Tbsp tapioca starch

1 tsp cinnamon
1 tsp soy lecithin powder
¼ tsp baking powder
½ tsp salt

Wet Ingredients:
2 Tbsp canola oil
1/3 c honey
1 Tbsp rice milk

1 Tbsp lemon juice
½ tsp vanilla extract

Additional Ingredients:
2/3 c O cereal (any cold cereal of oat O's that fits your taste and allergy needs)
1/3 c tightly packed chopped (into pieces the size of 1/3 to ½ of a dime) unsulphered dried apricots
1 Tbsp oat flour

Preheat oven to 300°F. Oil a 10 ½ by 7 ½ inch baking dish (slight size variations are fine if you don't have that size).

Place dry ingredients in mixing bowl and mix with fork.

Place wet ingredients in a different mixing bowl.

Put chopped apricots on a plate. Toss the Tbsp oat flour over them, and use fingers to separate slices to coat with flour.

Using an electric mixer, mix the wet ingredients on low for 15 seconds and then on high for 1 minute.

Pour wet mixture into dry and fold until almost blended.

Add apricots and O's and fold until just mixed.

Spread evenly in baking dish.

Bake for 40 minutes. Place pan on cooling rack.

After about a minute, use a metal spatula to slice into serving size pieces. Let cool in pan.

Apricot Oat Trail Bars
(for a firmer consistency, like granola bars)

Follow recipe for Apricot Oat Bars through the 40 minutes of baking. When removing pan from oven, increase oven temperature to 350°F. After bars are sliced, return to oven for 15 minutes. Set pan onto cooling rack for 5 minutes. Then remove individual bars and cool on cooling rack.

[Oa, Ri, GF*]

Bradley Bars
(Yes, my son's creation. 12 chewy, yummy bars)

Preheat oven to 325°F. Oil an 8" x 8" square cake pan.

Dry Ingredients:
1 1/4 c oat flakes (old fashioned)   ½ c barley flour
1/3 c raisins   ¼ c oat flour
¼ c sugar   ¼ c turbinado sugar
2 Tbsp tapioca starch   1 Tbsp rice flour
1 Tbsp rice bran   1 tsp xanthan gum
1/2 tsp baking soda

Wet Ingredients:
1/3 c canola oil   1/3 c agave syrup
2 Tbsp rice milk   ½ tsp vanilla extract

Put all dry ingredients except oat flakes and raisins into a bowl and mix well. Add oat flakes and raisins and mix.
Put wet ingredients into a bowl and blend thoroughly.
Pour wet into dry and fold until barely blended.
Spread evenly in baking pan, and then bake for 32 minutes.
Let cool 5 minutes on cooling rack. Then use a firm spatula to loosen around edges of pan and to cut bars into 12 pieces (or to desire size). Let cool in pan.

Chocolate Brownies

Dry Ingredients:
1 ½ c white spelt (or barley) flour
2/3 c white spelt (or oat) flour
1 c sugar
¼ c tapioca flour
¼ c cocoa powder
4 tsp tapioca starch
2 tsp baking powder
1 tsp salt

Wet Ingredients:
2/3 c canola (or safflower) oil
¼ c maple syrup
2 tsp vanilla extract

Additional Ingredients:
½ c rice milk
1 c chocolate chips

Preheat oven to 350°F. Oil a 12" x 9" (or similar) baking pan.
Mix dry ingredients in a bowl, sift once and set aside.
Put wet ingredients in a bowl and set aside.
Over very low heat, melt the chocolate chips with the rice milk, stirring constantly until smooth. Add the wet ingredients and stir. Turn off heat and let cool from hot to warm (about 10 minutes).
Pour wet into dry, and fold gently until just mixed.
Spread into pan, with slightly less batter along the edges than in the middle.
Bake 40 minutes (spelt) - 42 minutes (barley and oats), until top has crusted over. Let cool in pan on cooling rack. Slice when cool.

Optional: For a truly decadent, rich chocolate dessert, frost brownies with Chocolate Spread (see page 118).

Raisindoras

(These are like chocolate-free brownies, with a taste similar to Hermits. They are fun to prepare, and make great snacks!)

1 8 ½" by 6 ½" (or similar) baking pan

Boiling Ingredients:
1 c raisins
½ c sugar
½ c water
1 tsp cinnamon
¼ tsp cloves
¼ tsp nutmeg
½ tsp salt

Next Ingredient:
1 tsp baking soda

Final Ingredients:
1/3 c safflower oil
2 Tbsp apple sauce
1 c spelt (or other) flour

Put "boiling ingredients" into a small pot. Stir and cover. Bring to boil, uncover, and reduce heat to medium/low. Gently boil for 4 minutes, stirring occasionally. Remove from heat.

Gather any interested children to watch the next step!

Add the baking soda, and watch the mixture immediately turn white and frothy. Stir briefly and cover.

Let sit for 2 hours.

Five minutes before the two hours is done, preheat oven to 325°F.

Oil and flour baking pan.

Add final ingredients (wet ones first) and fold in until just mixed.

Spread evenly in pan. Bake for 50 minutes.

Sweet Cranberry Crisps

Pre-heat oven to 325°F. Lightly oil an 8" x 10" baking pan.

Dry Ingredients:

1 c + 2 Tbsp white rice flour ½ tsp baking soda
¼ c potato starch ½ tsp cream of tartar
¼ c tapioca flour ½ tsp salt
1 c sugar ¼ tsp baking powder

Wet Ingredients:

1/3 c honey 2 Tbsp lemon juice
1/4 c safflower oil

Additional Ingredients:

3 c crispy rice cereal 1/3 c dried cranberries*
2 Tbsp tahini or other seed butter if allergies permit (optional)

In a large bowl, mix together dry ingredients with fork.
Add the rice cereal and cranberries and mix.
Put wet ingredients into a bowl and mix.
Pour wet into dry, and mix thoroughly. Mixture will be crumbly like granola, not like a dough.
Spread in baking pan and then press down firmly over the entire surface (a hand pushing on the spatula end of a soft spatula works well) to tightly pack the dough. Bake for 35 minutes.
Place pan on cooling rack to cool.
After 20 minutes, use a firm spatula to loosen edges. After 45 minutes, use spatula to slice into portions. Leave bars in pan to cool.

*Other fruit options: You might also try dried blueberries, dried raspberries, or chopped dried apricots. (Note: Dried apricots get their orange color from a process that leaves metabisulphites, a common allergen, in the fruit. If this is a concern, use organic dried apricots, which will have an almost brown color.)

Banana Chip Cookies
(makes 2 dozen small cookies, or 1 dozen large cookies)

Dry Ingredients:
2/3 c sugar
½ c white rice flour
¼ c sorghum flour
2 Tbsp potato starch
1 ½ tsp tapioca starch
½ tsp soy lecithin powder
½ tsp baking powder
¼ tsp baking soda
¼ tsp xanthan gum
¼ tsp salt

Wet Ingredients:
¼ c safflower oil
2 Tbsp rice milk
1/3 c plus 1 Tbsp (i.e., a slightly rounded 1/3 c) banana, tightly packed (approximately 2 small/medium bananas)
½ tsp vanilla extract

Additional Ingredients:
½ c chocolate chips

Mix dry ingredients together. Sift 3 times, and set aside.

Put wet ingredients in blender. Blend on low speed for 15 seconds, then on high for 1 minute.

Pour wet into dry, and fold gently until almost mixed. Add the chocolate chips and fold gently until just mixed.

These cookies will come out best if the batter is refrigerated before baking – a couple of hours or even overnight. The result will be a cookie that will hold its thickness better. Also, the rice flour will feel less grainy, and the cookie itself will be slightly crunchier. However, if you do not have time to chill the batter, the cookies will still be good. Once the batter is chilled, the cookies can be made fresh, or the batter can be rolled and frozen for later slice and bake!

Pre-heat oven to 350°F. Oil 2 medium cookie sheets or one large cookie sheet.

For small cookies, use small spoon to place batter portions onto cookie sheet. Flatten slightly, and bake 18 - 20 minutes, until the edges of the cookies are slightly brown. For large cookies (3 – 3 ½"), use a rounded tablespoon, don't flatten, and bake for 25 minutes.

Transfer immediately to cookie rack to cool.

Eat warm, room temperature, or frozen!

Bunuelos
(makes 5 Mexican sweet treats much like fried dough)

Ingredients:
1 Tbsp sugar
1 tsp cinnamon
1 c spelt flour
½ tsp salt
2 Tbsp safflower oil
1/3 c cold water
High temperature safflower or canola oil for frying
¼ c honey

Mix the cinnamon with the sugar and set aside.

Mix the flour and salt. Cut in the oil with a knife (or fork). Gradually add the water, mixing as you add.

Knead the dough for 4 minutes on a lightly floured cutting board or table, adding occasional tiny amounts of flour if needed to prevent hands from sticking to dough.

Divide into 5 balls. Roll each ball very thin. (You can pick it up and let it stretch thinner with your hands much like you would with pizza dough.) Each piece will be 4 – 5 inches wide.

Heat ½" to ¾" deep of oil to 350°F- 375°F in a deep pan. (The pan should be at least an inch taller than the top of the oil, to limit splatter.)

One at a time, fry each piece in the oil, cooking on each side until golden (about a minute per side).

Remove with spatulas and place on absorbent paper towels.

While the second one is cooking, finish preparation of the first while it is still hot: Sprinkle with the cinnamon sugar and then drizzle almost a tablespoon of honey over the top of each. Repeat with the other four. Do not cover.

Serve right away while still hot, with one for each person.

Quick Bunuelos
(makes 5 large Mexican sweet treats much like fried dough)

Ingredients:
2 Tbsp sugar
2 tsp cinnamon
High temperature safflower or canola oil for frying
5 large spelt tortillas*
1/3 c honey

Mix the cinnamon with the sugar and set aside. Heat ½" to ¾" deep of oil to 350°F- 375°F in a wide, deep pan. (The pan should be at least an inch taller than the top of the oil, to limit splatter.) Lower a tortilla into the oil and cook on each side until golden (about a minute), turning with two spatulas – one on each side of the tortilla. Remove with spatulas and place on absorbent paper towels. While the second tortilla is cooking, finish preparation of the first while it is still hot: Sprinkle with cinnamon sugar and then drizzle about a tablespoon of honey over the top of each tortilla. Repeat with the remaining tortillas. Do not cover. Serve right away while still hot, with one tortilla for each person.

* If no wheat allergy, wheat tortillas can be used. Also possible are rice or corn tortillas. If using corn tortillas, reduce honey to ¼ c, sugar to 1 Tbsp, and cinnamon to 1 tsp to adjust for the corn tortillas' smaller size.

Many have asked if the actual recipes for Gak's Snacks boxed Chocolate Chip and Brownie Chip Cookies would be in the cookbook. Although we decided not to have our actual recipes in the cookbook, you will find here several variations of them. You can also use our very own delicious natural chocolate chips and natural cocoa powder, made in a facility free of peanuts or tree nuts, and not made on shared lines with dairy, available at our web store at www. gakssnacks.com.

Chocolate Chip Cookies
(makes 2 – 3 dozen crunchy small/medium cookies)

Dry Ingredients:
1 c white spelt flour (or white rice flour for gluten free)
½ c whole (or white) spelt flour (or 1/3 c sorghum flour & 1/8 c brown rice flour for gluten free)

¾ c sugar   ½ tsp baking powder
1 ½ tsp tapioca starch   ½ tsp salt
1 tsp baking soda   ½ tsp xanthan gum
1 tsp soy lecithin powder

Wet Ingredients:
1/3 c safflower oil
1/3 c plus 1 Tbsp rice milk (or ½ c for gluten free)
2 Tbsp apple sauce
1 tsp vanilla extract

Extra Ingredient:
½ c chocolate chips

    Preheat oven to 350°F. Oil 2 small (or one large) cookie sheets. Mix dry ingredients together, and sift 3 times.

    Put wet ingredients in blender. Blend on low speed for 15 seconds and then on high for 1 minute.

    Pour wet into dry, and fold gently until almost mixed. Add the chocolate chips and fold gently until just mixed. (For gluten free, best if batter is refrigerated for at least 2 hours before baking.)

    Spoon small portions of batter onto cookie sheet. Leave space between the cookies to allow spreading, and for crunchy cookies. (Extra batter can be refrigerated or frozen.) Bake 18 - 20 minutes (18 for gluten free). After 1 minute, transfer to cookie rack to cool. (If gluten free, best when fully cooled.)

Chocolate Chocolate Chip Cookies

Soft Chocolate Chocolate Chip Cookies [Sp]
(makes 2 - 3 dozen cookies)

These are actually, truly, the original Gak's Snacks brownie chip cookie! They were so delicious that we were encouraged to offer them outside of our family, friends, and school. However, they had always been eaten so quickly that we hadn't realized that they were too moist to be packaged. So, we made a new delicious recipe for our boxes, and offer our original recipe to you.

Dry Ingredients:
1 c white spelt flour
½ c whole spelt flour
1 c sugar
1/3 c cocoa powder
1 ½ tsp tapioca starch
1 tsp baking soda
1 tsp soy lecithin powder
½ tsp baking powder
½ tsp salt
½ tsp xanthan gum

Wet Ingredients:
1/3 c safflower oil
½ c rice milk
¼ c apple sauce
1 ½ tsp vanilla extract

Extra Ingredient:
½ c chocolate chips

Preheat oven to 350°F.

Oil 2 small (or one large) cookie sheets.

Mix dry ingredients together. Sift 3 times, and set aside.

Put wet ingredients in blender. Blend on low speed for about 15 seconds and then on high for about 45 seconds.

Pour wet into dry, and fold gently until almost mixed. Add the chocolate chips and fold gently until just mixed. The batter will be very wet.

Use a measuring teaspoon to place batter portions onto cookie sheet. (Extra batter can be refrigerated or even frozen to be cooked later! These will make thicker, softer cookies.) Leave space between the cookies to allow spreading. Bake 18 - 19 minutes. Let cool for about 1 minute on pan and then transfer to cookie rack to cool.

Eat when warm or cooled. If, by chance, you don't use them all up right away and need to put some away, put wax paper between the cookies so they don't stick together. These cookies will soften further in a zip-lock bag.

The following chocolate batter can be made into a few different kinds of cookies, as you will see in the recipe variations that follow it. With chips, it makes **Chocolate Chocolate Chip Cookies**. Without chips, you can make large **Crunchy Chocolate Cookies** or tiny **Chocolate Wafer Cookies** – or perhaps some of each with the same batter! The large chocolate cookies are absolutely delicious made into a sandwich filled with jam: **Chocolate Jam Sandwich Cookies**. Or, perhaps make large chocolate cookies, grind them up into crumbs, and use them to make an ice cream cake, and then use some wafer cookie as part of the cake's decoration.

Crunchy Chocolate Chocolate Chip Cookies
(makes 2 - 3 dozen cookies)

Dry Ingredients:
1 1/3 c white spelt flour
¼ c whole spelt flour
1 c sugar
1/3 c cocoa powder
2 Tbsp tapioca flour
1 tsp soy lecithin powder
½ tsp baking soda
½ tsp baking powder
½ tsp salt
½ tsp cream of tartar

Wet Ingredients:
1/3 c safflower oil
2/3 c rice milk
1 tsp vanilla extract

Additional Ingredient:
½ c chocolate chips

Preheat oven to 375°F.

Oil 2 small (or one large) cookie sheets.

Mix dry ingredients together. Sift 2 times, and set aside.

Put wet ingredients into a measuring cup (measure them directly into a glass measuring cup for easy cleaning!) or small bowl and stir.

Pour wet into dry, and fold gently until about ¾ mixed. Add chips gradually while folding. Fold until just mixed.

Use eating teaspoon to place batter portions onto cookie sheet. (Extra batter can be refrigerated or even frozen to be cooked later.) Leave space between the cookies to allow spreading. Use wet fingers to make portions round and then to flatten to ¼ thick. Bake 15 minutes. Immediately transfer cookies to cookie rack to cool.

Crunchy Chocolate Cookies

[Sp]

Follow directions for Crunchy Chocolate Chocolate Chip Cookies (p. 67) but leave out the chocolate chips. These are good ground up for the bottom of (R)ice cream cake (see page 99).

[Sp]

Chocolate Wafer Cookies

Follow recipe for Crunchy Chocolate Chocolate Chip Cookies (see page 67) without the chocolate chips.

Chill dough for at least 2 hours.

Scoop a slightly rounded measuring teaspoonful of dough for each cookie portion. Use wet fingers to make round and then to flatten to 1/8" thick. Cookie dough portions should resemble half dollars in size, shape, and thickness.

Bake at 375°F for 8 minutes, and immediately remove with spatula onto cooling rack.

[Sp]

Chocolate Jam Sandwich Cookies
(One of our favorites - great for a pot luck or a bake sale)

Follow directions for Crunchy Chocolate Chocolate Chip Cookies (see page 67) but leave out the chocolate chips. When cookies are cool, spread a thin layer of strained raspberry (our favorite), cherry, or apricot jam on the backs of half the cookies, and cover with the backs of the remaining cookies to make jam sandwiches.

Alternate: For real decadence, try this *with* the chocolate chips!

Cranberry Oatmeal Cookies
(makes a dozen large cookies)

Dry Ingredients:

1 ¾ c old fashioned oat flakes	1 Tbsp tapioca starch
¾ c oat flour	1 tsp baking powder
¼ c oat bran	1 tsp cream of tartar
1/3 c sugar	½ tsp salt
1/3 c brown sugar (measure tightly packed, and then loosen)	

Wet Ingredients:

½ c canola (or safflower) oil
¼ c orange juice
2 Tbsp maple syrup or 1 Tbsp syrup and 1 Tbsp molasses

Additional Ingredients:

¾ c fresh (or dried or frozen) cranberries

Mix together dry ingredients thoroughly with fork.

Put wet ingredients into a bowl or measuring cup, and mix.

Pour wet into dry, and fold two or three times. Gradually add cranberries while continuing to fold until just mixed.

Chill for at least 2 hours (if possible).

Pre-heat oven to 350°F. Oil large cookie sheet.

Use a large spoon to scoop portions onto cookie sheet, leaving room to spread, and leaving the shape as a round, high mound. Bake 17-18 minutes (16 for smaller cookies) or until edges of cookies are starting to brown. Place cookie sheet on cooling rack for 5 minutes. Then transfer cookies to cookie rack to cool the rest of the way.

Hint: If you have leftover cookies, leave them overnight in a baggie. In the morning, break them up into a bowl for instant granola! For more, try making Cranberry Granola (see page 28).

Alternate: For a softer, more floury cookie, decrease oat flakes to 1 ¼ c, and increase oat flour to 1 ¼ c. Bake for 17 minutes.

Donut Cookies
(makes about 2 ½ dozen cookies)

Part of the fun of experimenting with your own recipes can be when the result isn't at all what you had hoped for! When I was working on my donut recipe, one batch came out heavier than I would like. Rather than continuing to put the donut batter into the oil anyway, I decided to bake the last few chunks of batter. The result became this recipe! The baked donuts make terrific tea cookies!

Extra tools needed:
One extra bowl in which dough can rise
Two light dish towels for covering rising dough
One small pot for heating wet ingredients
One baking thermometer
Two large cookie trays
One rolling pin
One 2 ¼ inch donut cutter (If you can't get one, use 2 round cookie cutters, each a different size, or, if that is not possible, use a the top of a floured drinking cup for the outer circle, and then cut out a middle circle the size of a quarter with the tip of a spoon.)
Plastic wrap

Dry Ingredients:
2 c white spelt flour
1 c sugar
2/3 c + 2 tsp potato starch
¼ c arrowroot flour
1 ½ tsp yeast
1 ¼ tsp cinnamon
¼ tsp cloves
¼ tsp ginger
¼ tsp salt
¼ tsp nutmeg

Wet Ingredients:

¾ c apple cider (or apple juice)
¼ c safflower oil
½ c rice milk
2 Tbsp water
½ tsp vanilla

Additional Ingredients, with each being approximate amounts:

1. 1 ¼ c whole or white spelt flour
2. 1 Tbsp white spelt flour
3. 1 c white spelt flour
4. 2 tsp safflower oil
5. ¼ c white spelt flour

Mix dry ingredients well with fork, and set aside until at room temperature.

Put wet ingredients into a small pot. Stirring occasionally, heat to approximately 125°F.

(If it gets too hot, let sit to cool to 125°F. Pouring it out of the hot pot will facilitate cooling.)

Add wet ingredients to dry ingredients and mix with a spatula.

Using an electric mixer, mix on medium speed for 4 minutes. The batter will be very stretchy and sticky.

Clean off the dough from the mixer whisks into the batter.

Add "additional ingredient" #1, the 1 ¼ c whole spelt flour, and stir in with spatula.

Spread the "additional ingredient" #2, the 1 T whole spelt flour, over a cutting board or smooth table.

Knead the dough on that surface for about 6 minutes. (That means pushing down and a little bit forward on the dough a few times with the balls of your hands, using the weight of your body, while standing up, and then folding the dough over towards you to make it thick again, and repeating.) Any time a spot is sticky, add a tablespoon or two of the "additional ingredient" #3, ¾ c whole spelt flour, to the sticky area. You may need a bit more or less than the 1 cup. When through, the dough should be soft and springy and no longer sticky. End with the dough in a slightly flattened ball shape.

Place the "additional ingredient" #4, 2 tsp oil, into a mixing bowl, oiling the bowl, and leaving the remaining oil in the bottom of the bowl. Place the dough ball in the bowl, and roll it over until the dough is greased. Cover the bowl with a thick damp dish towel, and put the bowl in a warm (80°F to 85°F if possible), non-drafty place for 40 minutes. (One way to achieve something close to this is to turn on the oven, turn it off when it reaches 100°F, and put it in there, leaving the oven off.)

While the dough is rising, clean any stuck dough off the kneading area, and then lightly flour it again with about 1 tsp of the flour from "additional ingredient" #5, so that it is ready for later.

Oil the cookie sheets.

When the dough is ready, you ought to be able to leave a deep impression if you stick a couple of fingers deep into the dough. Otherwise, leave for a few more minutes.

In the bowl, punch down dough (about 20 punches) to get rid of any air. Then break dough into three pieces. Place the first piece on the prepared kneading area. Roll the dough into a round shape 1/3 - ½ an inch thick. Cut with the donut cutter, placing the cutter right to the edge of the dough, moving all around the circle. There should be approximately enough dough for 6 donuts on the outer rim and one in the middle. Carefully remove the inner circle from each donut, and place (trying not to stretch it) onto the cookie sheets. Set scrap pieces aside. Use another teaspoon of the flour (extra ingredient #5) to re-flour the area to repeat the process with the other two pieces of dough. Then take all scrap pieces, form a ball, and roll it, repeating the process.

Cover dough with plastic wrap, and then place a light dish towel over that. Again put in a warm non-drafty location and let rise for about an hour – a finger pushing on a donut should leave an indentation. When the hour is almost over, preheat the oven to 400°F. When the dough is ready, remove the towels and plastic wrap. Use an oil spray to spray the tops of the cookies. Bake for 20 minutes, or until golden brown.

Gingerbread People
(makes 2 dozen 3″ gingerbread people)

Pre-heat oven to 350°F. Oil large cookie sheet.

Dry Ingredients:

¾ c white rice flour*

¾ c tapioca flour

2/3 c sugar

1 ¼ tsp ginger

1 tsp soy lecithin powder

1 tsp yeast

½ tsp xanthan gum

½ tsp salt

¼ tsp cinnamon

¼ tsp cloves

Wet Ingredients:

1/3 c safflower oil

1/3 c rice milk

3 Tbsp molasses

Additional Ingredients:

¾ c buckwheat flour* (may contain small amount of gluten)

1 ¼ c white rice flour*

Rice flour for flouring surfaces*

Raisons, currents, dried cranberries, or other dried fruit for decorating people

Mix together dry ingredients with fork and set aside.

In a small bowl, mix the additional ¾ c buckwheat flour with the additional 1 c white rice flour, and set aside.

Put the first two wet ingredients into a small pot. Dip a measuring tablespoon into the mixture to "grease" it. Then use that spoon to measure the molasses into the pot.

Heat to 125°F (120°F – 130°F is fine). If you do not have a thermometer, this is very hot to the touch but not burning hot. Note: This goes very quickly – about half a minute on low, so keep a close eye on it. If you do overheat it, transfer it to a different bowl to cool.

Pour wet into dry. Mix with a spatula until the flour is mostly integrated into the mixture. Then mix with electric beaters on medium speed for 4 minutes. Turn off and scrape any loose dough off the beaters into the bowl.

Add about 1/3 c of the "additional ingredient" flour, blending it into the mixture with a spatula. Add as much of the flour as is needed to produce a thick, not very sticky mixture.

Lightly flour a smooth surface (this can be the bowl), and knead the dough for 6 minutes (see Donuts, page 22, for more detailed explanation), adding more of the flour as needed to keep the dough from sticking to your hands or the surface you are kneading on. The resulting dough will be thick and dense.

Place dough in bowl covered with a towel in a warm, non-drafty spot for 40 minutes.

Punch out air, even though it is unlikely to have risen appreciably, if at all. (Note: The goal with using yeast with the cookies is not to have them rise, but rather to have the dough hold together enough to make cut out cookies. That is also why the recipe calls for so little yeast.)

Oil and lightly flour a large cookie sheet or cutting board.

Roll out the dough to ¼" thick.

Use cookie cutter to make shapes, or design your own with a pointy knife. Place on oiled and lightly floured cookie sheet. Decorate with dried fruit pieces.

Bake 8 - 10 minutes. After cooling on pan for 2 minutes, remove to cooling rack.

Frost with Gingerbread Frosting (see page 119).

*For a grainy texture, use recipe as written. For a smoother texture, substitute spelt flour for the rice and buckwheat flour as follows: Replace initial ¾ c rice flour with ¾ c whole spelt flour. Substitute additional 1 ¼ c rice flour and ¾ c buckwheat flour with 2 – 2 ¼ c white spelt flour. Use white spelt flour for flouring surfaces. For a soft cookie, bake 9 minutes. For a crunchy cookie, bake 15 minutes.

Ginger cookies
(makes 2 dozen cookies)

Pan Ingredients:
1/3 c canola oil
2 Tbsp chopped ginger
½ c brown sugar
1 tsp vanilla extract
¼ tsp cloves
¼ c rice milk

Dry Ingredients:
1 c whole spelt flour
1 c white spelt flour
1 Tbsp potato starch
1 tsp soy lecithin powder
1 tsp baking powder
½ tsp baking soda
½ tsp xanthan gum
½ tsp salt

Additional Ingredient:
¼ c raisins

Preheat oven to 350°F, and oil large cookie tray.

Heat a pan on the stove. Add oil. When hot, add ginger and turn heat to medium low. Sauté, stirring steadily, until the ginger has begun to lightly brown. Add brown sugar and stir until sugar has blended and begun to dissolve. Turn off heat and add vanilla, cloves, and rice milk. Stir, and set aside.

Mix dry ingredients and sift twice.

Pour the wet ingredients into the dry, and fold gently until almost blended. Add raisins and fold until barely blended.

Spoon out onto cookie sheet. Flatten to about 1/3 inch thick quickly with fork. Bake 23 minutes.

Hamentashen
(makes about 1 ½ dozen three-cornered cookies)

1 large or 2 medium cookie sheets

Dry Ingredients:
2 ¾ c white spelt flour
1 c sugar
1/3 c potato starch
1 ½ tsp yeast
¼ tsp salt

Wet Ingredients:
½ c water
½ c safflower oil
2 Tbsp orange juice

Additional Ingredients:
White spelt flour (likely about ¼ c)
safflower oil (a bit of spray or a few teaspoons)

Prune Filling:
2/3 c water
¾ c dried pitted chopped prunes
¼ c raisins
½ c sugar
2 Tbsp honey
2 tsp lemon juice
Combine in pot, stir, and cover. Heat on medium/low for 10 minutes. Let cool for 10 minutes and puree in food processor or blender.

Or, Apricot Filling:
2/3 c water
1 c dried chopped apricots (unsulphered/organic, in order to avoid

metabisulphates, a common allergen. Unsulphered apricots are an orange brown, rather than bright orange.)

2/3 c sugar

2 Tbsp honey

1 Tbsp orange juice

Combine in pot, stir, and cover. Heat on medium/low for 10 minutes. Let cool for 10 minutes and puree in food processor or blender.

Or, Quick Filling:

Your favorite jam (apricot, rasberry, or cherry work best)

Mix dry ingredients well with fork, and set aside until at room temperature.

Put wet ingredients into a small pot. Stirring occasionally, heat to approximately 125°F. (If it gets too hot, let sit to cool to 125°F. Pouring it out of the hot pot will facilitate cooling.)

Add wet ingredients to dry, mixing with a fork until the wet ingredients are absorbed, and then kneading in the bowl with hands until remaining flour is absorbed into the dough.

Lightly flour a flat surface, and knead the dough for about 7 additional minutes. (See page 22, the Donut recipe, for more on kneading.) If at any time a spot is sticky, add a bit of the "additional ingredient" flour. End with the dough in a slightly flattened ball shape.

Spray bottom of bowl with oil (or just oil it). Place the dough ball in the bowl, and spray it with oil (or roll it in the oil in the bowl). Cover the bowl with a thick damp dish towel, and put the bowl in a warm (80°F to 85°F if possible), non-drafty place for 40 minutes. (One way to achieve something close to this is to turn on the oven for less than a minute and turn it off again, and then place the dough in there.)

While the dough is rising, clean any stuck dough off the kneading area, and then lightly flour it again.

Cover cookie sheets with parchment paper (or oil them).

In the bowl, punch down dough (about 20 punches) to get rid of any air. Then break dough into three pieces. Roll each piece to 1/4" thick on the lightly floured surface. Using a round cookie cutter (or drinking cup), cut out circles 3" to 4" wide. Use the scraps to form and roll a final ball.

Very lightly dab (with wet fingers) the outer half inch or so of each circle with cold water. (This will help sides stick together). Dot center of the circle with a small spoonful of filling (less than a measuring teaspoonful).

Fold up circle on 3 sides (forming a triangle), pinching sides tightly together, leaving only a small open spot (about ½") in the center to view the filling.

Lightly cover cookies with plastic wrap. Again place in warm non-drafty location and let rise for 45 - 60 minutes. (If your hamentashen are rising in the oven, be sure to remove them from there before the next step!) When the hour is almost over, set oven rack to slightly higher than the middle of the oven, and preheat oven to 375°F. When the dough is ready, remove the plastic wrap. Re-pinch the three corners on any cookie that doesn't have a very pinched look. Use an oil spray (or brush) to spray the tops of the cookies. Bake for 25-30 minutes until lightly golden. Slide parchment paper with hamentashen onto cooling rack.

Jam Cookies
(These aren't meant to be picture perfect. They're for being fun to make with kids, and yummy to eat! Makes 24 cookies.)

Pre-heat oven to 350°F. Oil 2 muffin tins (yes, really, muffin tins!)

Dry Ingredients:
2/3 c white spelt flour   ½ tsp xanthan gum
1/3 c whole spelt flour   ½ tsp baking powder
½ c sugar   ½ tsp salt
1 tsp soy lecithin powder   ¼ tsp baking soda
1 tsp potato starch (optional)

Wet Ingredients:
¼ c safflower oil   1 ½ tsp vanilla extract
¼ c rice milk   2 Tbsp apple sauce (or apple cherry
                        or apple blackberry sauce!)

Extra Ingredient:
½ c jam (blackberry, raspberry, blueberry, or cherry, or assortment)

Mix together dry ingredients with fork, sift 3 times, and set aside.

Put wet ingredients in blender. Blend on low speed for about 15 seconds and then on high for about a minute.

Pour wet into dry and fold gently until just mixed.

Place small batter portions into muffin tins. Wet fingers with cold water. Quickly, use 2 finger tips of each hand to pat down batter to somewhat flatten it. A few quick prods are sufficient; the batter does not have to reach the edges, since it will settle in when heated.

With a small spoon, press 1 tsp of jam into and across the center of each cookie. Push at least some of it lower than the rest of the batter (while not going through the batter to the pan). This will enable some of the batter to spread and cook over some of the jam.

Bake 20 minutes.

Immediately transfer cookies to cookie rack to cool.

Maple Raisin Cookies
(makes 18 large cookies)

Here in New England, as the autumn leaves turn brilliant colors, the maple syrup is tapped. These cookies capture the maple flavor of the season. Serve these cookies anytime, but they are especially timely for fall holidays and parties.

Dry Ingredients:

1 1/8 c (1 c plus 2 Tbsp) barley flour
1/3 c tapioca starch
2 Tbsp oat (or rice) flour
2/3 c sugar
1 tsp soy lecithin powder

1 tsp cream of tartar
½ tsp xanthan gum
½ tsp baking soda
½ tsp baking powder
¼ tsp salt

Wet Ingredients:

1/3 c safflower oil
2 Tbsp pear juice (or apple juice)
1/3 c maple syrup

Additional Ingredients:

½ c raisins (small size)

Pre-heat oven to 375°F. Oil large cookie sheet.

Mix dry ingredients with fork. Add raisins, mix, and set aside.

Put wet ingredients into a bowl. Stir with a fork.

Pour wet into dry. Fold gently with spatula just until the flour is incorporated.

Chill in refrigerator for 2 hours or longer. (Overnight is fine.)

Spoon ball-shaped portions of approximately 1 inch each onto cookie sheet at least 3 inches apart to allow for spreading.

Bake 11- 12 minutes until very lightly browned. (For a very crunchy cookie, bake for 15-16 minutes.) Place cookie sheet on stove top or cooling rack for 2 - 3 minutes. Then transfer cookies to cookie rack to cool the rest of the way.

Oatmeal Raisin Cookies (replacement of recipe in cookbook, p. 81)
(makes 18 cookies)

Dry Ingredients:

1 c oat flakes (old fashioned)

1 ¼ c oat flour

½ c sugar

¼ c brown sugar (tightly packed)

1 Tbsp tapioca starch

½ tsp baking powder

¼ tsp baking soda

½ tsp cream of tartar

½ tsp salt

Wet Ingredients:

1/3 c canola (or safflower) oil

2 Tbsp apple sauce

1 Tbsp water

1 Tbsp maple syrup (preferably grade B)

1 Tbsp molasses

½ tsp vanilla extract

Additional Ingredients:

½ c raisins (small size)

Pre-heat oven to 350°F. Oil 2 large cookie sheets.

Mix dry ingredients with fork. Add raisins, mix, and set aside.

Put wet ingredients into a bowl. Beat with a fork until smooth.

Pour wet into dry, and fold until just mixed.

These can be baked right away or chilled first. (Chilled will produce a slightly softer cookie.)

Use a spoon to scoop portions onto cookie sheet, and use fingers if needed to shape as a round, high mound. Bake 17-18 minutes (add a minute if refrigerated first) or until edges of cookies are starting to lightly brown. Place cookie sheet on cooling rack for 5 minutes. Then transfer cookies to cookie rack to cool the rest of the way.

[Oa, GF*]

Oatmeal Raisin Cookies
(makes a dozen large cookies)

Dry Ingredients:
1 ¼ c oat flakes (old fashioned)
1 c oat flour
½ c sugar
1/3 c brown sugar (tightly packed)
1 Tbsp tapioca starch
1 tsp baking powder
½ tsp cream of tartar
½ tsp salt

Wet Ingredients:
½ c canola (or safflower) oil
2 Tbsp apple sauce
2 Tbsp water
1 Tbsp maple syrup (preferably grade B)
1 Tbsp molasses
½ tsp vanilla extract

Additional Ingredients:
½ c raisins (small size)

Pre-heat oven to 350°F. Oil large cookie sheet.
Mix dry ingredients with fork. Add raisins, mix, and set aside.
Put wet ingredients into a bowl. Beat with a fork until smooth.
Pour wet into dry, and fold until just mixed.
These can be baked right away or chilled first. (Chilled will produce a slightly softer cookie.)
Use a large spoon to scoop portions onto cookie sheet, leaving the shape as a round, high mound. Bake 15-16 minutes (add a minute if refrigerated first) or until edges of cookies are starting to lightly brown. Place cookie sheet on cooling rack for 5 minutes. Then transfer cookies to cookie rack to cool the rest of the way.

Cookies

81

Orange Raisin Cookies
(makes about 18 cookies - my son Bradley's invention!)

Dry Ingredients:
2/3 c sorgham flour
1/2 c white rice flour
¼ c brown rice flour
2/3 c sugar
1 Tbsp tapioca
1 Tbsp potato starch
1 1/2 tsp cinnamon
1 tsp soy lecithin powder
1 tsp baking soda
½ tsp xanthan gum

Wet Ingredients:
¼ c safflower (or canola) oil
¼ c agave syrup
¼ c orange juice
2 Tbsp apple sauce
1 tsp vanilla extract

Additional Ingredients:
1/3 c raisins (optional, small size)

Pre-heat oven to 350°F. Place parchment paper on large cookie sheet (or oil cookie sheet).

Mix dry ingredients with fork. Add raisins (if using) and mix.

Put wet ingredients into a bowl. Beat with a fork until smooth.

Pour wet into dry, and fold until just mixed.

These can be baked right away (9 at a time) or chilled first. (Chilled will produce a slightly softer cookie.)

Use small spoon to scoop portions onto cookie sheet.

Bake 14-15 minutes or until lightly browned. Slide parchment paper, with the cookies still on it, onto the cookie rack to cool .

Peachy Passover Cookies
(makes 24 small cookies)

Dry Ingredients:
1 1/3 c (3 ¼ pieces) spelt matza farfel. You can make your own farfel (i.e., very small broken matza pieces) by mashing matza with a potato masher in a bowl.
1/3 c tapioca flour
1/3 c potato starch
1/3 c sugar
1 tsp baking powder
½ tsp cinnamon
¼ tsp salt
¼ tsp ground ginger

Wet Ingredients:
1/3 c safflower oil
1 T apple juice
2 Tbsp apple sauce
2 Tbsp maple syrup
2 Tbsp peach preserves
1 ½ tsp vanilla extract
1 ½ tsp lemon juice

Mix together dry ingredients with fork. Set aside.
Mix wet ingredients with a fork.
Pour wet into dry, and fold gently until just mixed.
The cookies come out best if dough is refrigerated for at least two hours, but they can be baked immediately after mixing dough.
Pre-heat oven to 350°F. Oil cookie pan.
Handling dough as little as possible, shape into balls and then flatten slightly on tray.
Bake 20 minutes.
Remove from cookie sheet immediately, and transfer to cooling rack. Best when completely cooled (about an hour).

Sugar Cookies/Decorated Cookies
(crunchy cookies flavored with a hint of lemon)

Pre-heat oven to 350°F. Oil large cookie sheet.

Dry Ingredients:
½ c white spelt flour
½ c sugar
1/3 c white rice flour
¼ c potato starch
2 Tbsp tapioca starch
1 ½ tsp potato starch
1 tsp soy lecithin powder
1 tsp baking soda
½ tsp xanthan gum
½ tsp salt
½ tsp cream of tartar

Wet Ingredients:
¼ c lemon juice
1/3 c safflower oil
2 Tbsp apple sauce
1 Tbsp water
1 tsp vanilla extract
½ tsp lemon peel

Final Ingredient:
½ c powdered sugar, sifted

Optional Ingredient:
1/8 - 1/4 c sprinkles

Mix dry ingredients with a fork, sift 3 times, and set aside.

Put wet ingredients in blender. Blend on low speed for 15 seconds, then on high for 1 minute.

Pour wet into dry, and fold gently until just mixed. The batter will be very light and very soft.

Handling as little as possible, pull off small pieces with fingers or spoon. For any pieces that are not reasonably ball shaped, use hands to round out.

Place powdered sugar in a wide bowl or plate. For regular sugar cookies, roll the balls lightly in the powdered sugar, and place on cookie sheet.

Decorated Cookies/Christmas Cookies: For decorated cookies, pour colorful sprinkles over half of the powdered sugar. Roll one side of the cookie in the sprinkles, so that sprinkles and a bit of powdered sugar coat that side. Roll or flip over into the powdered sugar to coat the rest. Place on cookie sheet with sprinkle side up.

Bake 18-20 minutes or until edges of cookies are light brown. Place cookie sheet on cooling rack for 10 minutes. Then transfer cookies directly onto cooling rack to cool the rest of the way.

Vanilla Cookies
(makes 12 large cookies
with a subtle banana background flavor)

Dry Ingredients:
¾ c white rice flour
1/3 c quinoa flour
¾ c sugar
1 Tbsp tapioca flour
1 tsp baking powder
1 tsp soy lecithin powder
½ tsp xanthan gum
½ tsp salt

Wet Ingredients:
½ c safflower oil
1/3 c banana, tightly packed
1 Tbsp vanilla extract
1 Tbsp rice milk

Put dry ingredients in large mixing bowl. Mix thoroughly with fork, sift 3 times, and set aside.

Put wet ingredients in blender.

Preheat oven to 350°F. Oil cookie sheet.

Blend wet ingredients on low speed about 15 seconds, then high speed for about 15 seconds.

Pour wet into dry, and fold gently until almost mixed.

Spoon with heaping teaspoon into cookie sheets. Flatten slightly with fork. Bake for 30 minutes or until browned at the edges. Immediately remove from cookie sheets and cool on cooling rack.

Cake and Ice Cream

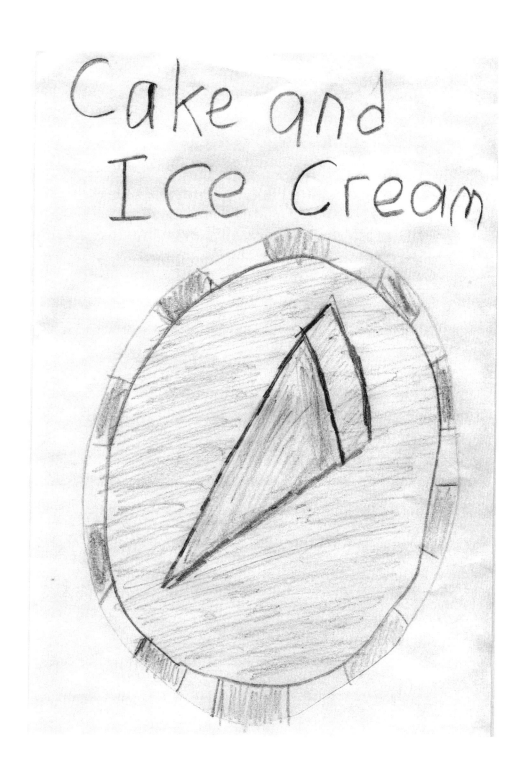

Birthday Cakes and Cupcakes

[Sp]

Chocolate Birthday Cake or Cupcakes
(makes two layers of cake or 2 dozen cupcakes -
like a "regular" cake, with a very light chocolate flavor.
We recently brought this cake with Creamy White Frosting (see
page 121) to a class party and everyone loved it.
One girl had a third helping.)

Dry Ingredients:
1 ¾ c white spelt flour
1 ¼ c sugar
2/3 c potato starch
1/3 c cocoa powder (or an extra Tbsp for a bit more chocolatey)
1 Tbsp tapioca starch
1 ½ tsp soy lecithin powder
1 tsp baking soda
1 tsp xanthan gum
½ tsp baking powder
½ tsp salt
¼ tsp cream of tartar

Wet Ingredients:
2/3 c safflower oil
¾ c pear juice (or apple juice)
2/3 c (tightly packed) ripe (or canned) Bartlett pear, peeled and
sliced (about 1 pear)
¼ c original rice milk
1 tsp vanilla extract

Additional Ingredient:
White spelt flour for flouring pans if making cake
Paper baking cups if making cupcakes

Sift the cocoa powder into a bowl. Add the rest of the dry ingredients and mix thoroughly. Sift 2 times.

Put wet ingredients in blender.

Let all ingredients warm to room temperature.

Pre-heat oven to 350°F. Fill 2 muffin tins with paper baking cups or oil and flour two 8" (or 9") cake pans for cake. Or, for cakes to be especially easy to remove (in one piece!) from pans, try cutting parchment paper to fit as exactly as possible onto the bottoms of the cake pans. Still lightly oil and flour the sides, but use the parchment paper on the bottoms.

Blend wet ingredients on low for about 15 seconds, then on high for about a minute.

Pour wet into dry and fold gently until just blended.

Then use an electric mixer on low for 15 seconds and then on high for 1 minute. If the dough is riding almost to the top of the mixer beaters, add a teaspoon or two of water and continue to mix.

Pour into cake pans. Immediately put into oven.

Cook cupcakes for 25 minutes, or cake for 35 minutes.

Let cool in pan on rack for 5 minutes. Then remove from pan and cool (right side up) on rack.

When completely cooled, frost. Try the Fudge Frosting (see page 118), the richness of which balances nicely with the light chocolate flavor of this cake, or the Creamy White Frosting (see page 121) for a lighter feel and a nice color contrast.

Rich Chocolate Cake or Cupcakes
(makes one thick layer of cake or two dozen cupcakes
of very rich, moist chocolate cake)

Dry Ingredients:
1 1/8 c (1 c plus 2 Tbsp) sugar

¾ c sorghum flour

2/3 c natural cocoa powder (If baking for very young children, you may want to reduce the cocoa to ½ c for a less rich cake.)

½ c white rice flour

1/3 c potato starch

1 Tbsp tapioca starch

1 ½ tsp soy lecithin powder

1 tsp xanthan gum

1 tsp baking powder

½ tsp baking soda

½ tsp salt

Wet Ingredients:
¾ c safflower oil

2/3 c apple sauce

2/3 c rice milk

1/3 c ripe banana (about ½ a medium banana)

1 tsp vanilla extract

Additional Ingredient:
White rice flour for flouring cake pan, or paper cups for muffin tins

Sift the cocoa powder into a bowl.

Add the rest of the dry ingredients and mix thoroughly. Sift 1 time.

Put wet ingredients in blender.

Let all ingredients warm to room temperature.

Pre-heat oven to 350°F. Oil and lightly flour cake pan, or line muffin pans with cupcake papers.

Blend wet ingredients on low for about 15 seconds, then on high for about a minute.

Pour wet into dry and fold gently until most of the flour is incorporated.

Then use an electric mixer for five minutes, starting on low and moving up steadily to high.

Pour into batter into the cake pan or muffin tins. For the cupcakes, fill cupcake liners half full. (The cupcakes will rise to the top of the paper.)

Bake for 50 minutes for cake or 30 minutes for cupcakes.

Let cool in pan on rack for 5 minutes. Then remove from pan and cool on rack.

When completely cooled, frost.

Optional: If you make a double recipe, this cake makes a Cherry Chocolate Cake by using Fruit (Cherry) Glaze (see page 124) between layers. Or you can make the single layer cake and spread cherry glaze over the top, and on the plate around the cake as well. You might even try slicing in half a single layer of cooled cake (by turning the cake slowly while cutting with a serrated knife), spreading cherry glaze over the cut top, and then putting the top half back on. Then you can drizzle Cherry Glaze over the top.

Vanilla Birthday Cake or Cupcakes
(makes one layer of cake or 1 dozen cupcakes)

Dry Ingredients:

1 c barley flour

¼ c oat flour (or sorghum – will make it a bit more like a corn
    muffin)

¼ c potato starch   ½ tsp baking soda

2 Tbsp tapioca flour   ½ tsp xanthan gum

1 tsp soy lecithin powder   ½ tsp cream of tartar

1 tsp baking powder   ½ tsp salt

Wet Ingredients:

¾ c sugar (yes, even though dry)   1/3 c apple sauce

½ c safflower oil   1 ½ tsp vanilla extract

½ c apple juice

Line a muffin tin with cupcake liners, or oil and flour (with barley flour) a 9" (or 8") round cake pan, or oil and flour sides and cut parchment paper to fit on the bottom. Parchment paper this way works great for removing the cake easily and in one piece, and keeps flour off what will become the top of the cake. I tip the pan over and trace the bottom on the parchment paper and then cut just inside the line.

Mix dry ingredients together, and sift 1 time.

Put wet ingredients into a bowl (preferably with a spout) for electric mixer. When room temperature, preheat oven to 350°F.

Mix wet ingredients on low for a few seconds and then on medium for 2 minutes. Turn beaters to low and gradually add the flour mixture (over about half a minute). When the flour is incorporated, mix on medium high for an additional 2 minutes.

Pour into cake pan or cupcake liners. Immediately put into oven.

Bake for 30 minutes for cupcakes, 35 minutes for cake.

Let cool in pan on rack for 5 minutes. Then remove from pan and cool on rack. When completely cooled, frost.

Vanilla Pear Birthday Cake or Cupcakes
(makes 24 cupcakes or a 2 layer cake)

This is an incredibly light, moist, "regular" cake-like cake.
We all had big smiles at our son's birthday party
when kids asked for seconds.

Pre-heat oven to 350°F. Put cupcake papers in two muffin tins, or oil and flour two 8" (or 9") cake pans, or oil and flour sides and cut parchment paper to fit as perfectly as possible on the bottom.

Dry Ingredients:
1 ¾ c white spelt flour
2/3 c potato starch
1 Tbsp tapioca starch
1 ½ tsp soy lecithin powder

1 tsp baking soda
1 tsp baking powder
1 tsp xanthan gum
½ tsp salt

Wet Ingredients:
¾ c pear juice (or apple juice)
2/3 c safflower oil
2/3 c (tightly packed) ripe (or canned) Bartlett pear, peeled and sliced (about 1 pear)

2 Tbsp lemon juice
1 ½ tsp vanilla extract
1 ¼ c sugar

Mix dry ingredients together with a fork, and sift 1 time.

Blend wet ingredients in blender on low for about 15 seconds, then on high for 1 minute.

Pour wet into dry and fold gently until most of the flour is incorporated. Mix with electric mixer on low for 15 seconds and then on high for 1 minute.

Pour into cupcake papers or cake pans. Immediately put into oven. Cook cupcakes for 25 minutes, or cakes for 35 minutes.

Let cool in pan on rack for 5 minutes, then directly on rack.

When completely cooled, frost. The Chocolate Frosting (see page 117) is delicious on this cake.

Yellow Birthday Cake and Cupcakes
(makes one two-layer cake or 2 dozen cupcakes)

2 9" (or 8") round cake pans, oiled and floured, or oiled and floured on sides and covered with cut out parchment paper on the bottom, or 2 muffin tins lined with paper cups.

Preheat oven to 350°F.

Dry Ingredients:
2 ¼ c spelt flour*
2/3 c sugar
¼ c potato starch
4 tsp tapioca starch
2 tsp soy lecithin powder
1 tsp baking powder
1 tsp xanthan gum
½ tsp baking soda
½ tsp salt

Wet Ingredients:
½ c additional sugar
½ c safflower oil
1/3 c apple sauce
¼ c apple juice
¼ c rice milk
¼ c water
4 tsp vanilla extract
2 tsp lemon juice

Thoroughly mix dry ingredients . Sift 1 time and set aside.

Put wet ingredients in mixer. Mix on low speed for about 15 seconds and then on high for about 45 seconds. Lower speed, and gradually add flour mixture while mixing, over about 30 seconds. Increase speed again, and continue mixing for 1 additional minute.

Pour into pans. Smooth with spatula so the batter is an even, thin layer - about ½".

Bake at 350°F for 32 minutes for cake, 26 minutes for muffins.

Let cool in pan on rack for 5 minutes. Then remove from pan and cool on rack. When completely cooled, frost.

*For barley flour option (which produces a light brown cake): Replace spelt flour and potato starch with 2 c barley flour and ½ c potato starch; Replace the ¼ c water with ½ c water, and decrease cooking time to 30 minutes.

For gluten free option (cake will be light brown), cook 1 - 2 minutes longer or use 9" pans, and use the following ingredients:

Dry Ingredients:
1 c white rice flour
½ c quinoi flour
½ c buckwheat flour
1 c sugar
½ c potato starch
1 Tbsp tapioca starch
2 tsp soy lecithin powder
1 tsp baking powder
1 ¼ tsp xanthan gum
½ tsp baking soda
½ tsp salt

Wet Ingredients:
½ c additional sugar
½ c safflower oil
1/3 c apple sauce
½ c apple juice
½ c rice milk
2 Tbsp vanilla extract
2 tsp lemon juice

Ice Cream Treats

Vanilla Rice Milk Ice Cream
(soft when first prepared, firm after freezing overnight)

Ingredients:
2 ½ c vanilla rice milk (chilled)
½ c safflower oil (chilled)
¾ c sugar
1 ¼ tsp vanilla extract (or almost 2 teaspoons if using regular, rather than vanilla, rice milk)
¼ tsp soy lecithin powder
¼ tsp salt
1 tsp guar gum (which may contain traces of soy) (or xanthan gum)

Put all the ingredients into a chilled mixing bowl. Beat with an electric mixer (or wisk) on medium/low for 2 minutes. Put in ice cream maker and follow directions of the ice cream maker. Note: Do not let ingredients sit for more than a couple of minutes prior to putting into the ice cream maker.

Optional: Add 2/3 c of your favorite mix-in to the batter during the last 5 minutes of mixing in the ice cream maker.

[GF]

Chocolate Rice Milk Ice Cream

Follow recipe for Vanilla Rice Milk Ice Cream (see above), but use chocolate rice milk, and reduce vanilla extract to 1 tsp. Try swirling in some Chocolate Sauce (see page 117) in the last few seconds.

Note: For those who eat soy, soy milk works well too. An equal mix of chocolate soy milk and vanilla rice milk makes a great ice cream!

Peach (or other fruit) Rice Milk Ice Cream

Follow recipe for Vanilla Rice Milk Ice Cream (see page 96), but use ¾ tsp vanilla. When the ice cream is 5 minutes from done in the ice cream maker, add 2/3 c chopped fresh or frozen peaches (or other fruit).

Chocolate Chip Cookie Ice Cream Sandwiches

Use Chocolate Chip Cookie recipe (see page 65), but add 2 Tbsp oil. Freeze. Between 2 cookies, spread some Rice Milk Ice Cream (see page 96). Refreeze if you prefer the ice cream firmer. Or use any ice cream/rice cream/soy cream as your allergies allow.

Ice Cream Sandwiches

Make Soft Chocolate Chocolate Chip Cookies (see page 64), with or without the chocolate chips as desired. Between 2 cookies, spread some Rice Milk Ice Cream (see page 96). Refreeze if you prefer the ice cream firmer, since it is quite soft out of the ice cream maker. Or use any ice cream/rice cream/soy cream, or even raspberry sorbet, as your allergies allow.

Garden Surprise

(This is a great recipe for kids - There is no right amount of any of the above ingredients, and no right order. Just have fun making an edible garden mixture.)

You Will Need:

1 large or several serving size dishes, chilled. (Glass is fun, since you can see inside.)

Crumbs from Crunchy Chocolate Cookies (see page 68) (or other favorite dirt or sand colored cookies)

Chocolate Rice Milk Ice Cream (see page 96) (or ice cream if allergies allow)

Gummy Worms

Perhaps you'll want to stick in a sprig of parsley as a plant. Or make a craft flower, wrap the bottom of the stem in plastic wrap, and plant it.

Combine, display, giggle, and eat.

(R)ice Cream Cake

1 10" springform pan, chilled in freezer until ready to fill

Cake Parts to Make in Advance:

Crunchy Chocolate Cookies (see page 68) (or other favorite cookies) enough to make about 1 c crumbs
1 layer of 9" round cake of your choosing (Note, although Chocolate Fudge Cake is great with ice cream, it is too dense a cake to dig into when frozen. Other cakes would therefore be preferable.)
Chocolate Sauce (see page 117) or Fruit Glaze (see page 124), if preferred

Cake Parts to Make During Cake Construction:

Vanilla Rice Milk Ice Cream (see page 96) (or ice cream if allergies allow)
A triple recipe of Fudge Frosting (see page 118) or Vanilla Fudge Frosting (see page 122) if preferred.

Optional Ingredients:

Decorations for top of cake

Blend cookies in food processor until they are crumbs (or blend 2 or 3 cookies at a time in a blender). Spread the cookie crumbs on bottom of springform pan. The layer of crumbs should be thick enough that you cannot see the bottom of the pan.

Line the edges of the springform pan with several pieces of plastic wrap, with enough of the top of the wrap sticking up over the top to make it easy to pull later.

Slice the top half of the cake off the bottom half of the cake. (Hint: turn the cake bit by bit while cutting with a serrated knife.) Thinly frost the open side of each half. Chill in freezer for 5 minutes so frosting hardens a bit. Then flip the halves over onto plastic wrap, frosting sides down, and frost the other sides as well. If you have enough fudge frosting, also frost the sides. Since only the top of the top half will show, it is fine if the frosting process is roughly done. (The frosting is not only for adding flavor and texture, but is also for protecting the cake from melting ice cream.)

Make rice milk ice cream. Spread ice cream over cookie crumbs right away while it is still soft by dropping small spoonfuls all over the crumbs. When mostly coated, carefully smooth out flat, also spreading some ½" to 1" up the sides of the pan.

Center the bottom half of the frosted cake on top of the ice cream layer.

Cover with plastic wrap and freeze for at least an hour.

When ready to proceed, make more ice cream. (Most standard ice cream makers, and therefore the recipe in this book, will only make enough at a time for ½ the ice cream needed for this cake.) Spread most of this ice cream over the cake surface as well as in any remaining space along the sides of the cake, saving enough for the similar space around the top cake layer. Cover with top ½ of cake. Fill the space around the edges with the remaining ice cream. Cover with plastic wrap and freeze, preferably minimally overnight – this ice cream gets harder when frozen longer.

When ready to serve, let thaw briefly. Slide out the plastic wrap. Push on the pan's base to push the cake through the pan.

Drizzle Chocolate Sauce (or Cherry Glaze) over top edges and down sides. Add any frosting decorations if desired.

Cakes for Entertaining and Holidays

[Ba, Oa, LNS]

Carrot Pineapple Cake
(a lightly sweetened cake with a subtle pineapple flavor)

Pre-heat oven to 350°F. Oil and flour an 8" x 8" square cake pan.

Dry Ingredients:
3/4 c barley flour

3/4 c oat flour

½ c turbinado (or white) sugar

1/3 c potato starch

1 tsp soy lecithin powder

1 tsp baking powder

½ tsp baking soda

½ tsp xanthan gum

¼ tsp salt

¼ tsp cloves

1/8 tsp nutmeg

Wet Ingredients:
1 8 oz. can crushed pineapple in juice

1/3 c safflower oil

1 tsp vanilla extract

Extra Ingredients:
¾ c (tightly packed) grated carrots

½ c raisins

Mix dry ingredients together, and sift 3 times.

Put wet ingredients in blender. Blend on low for about 15 seconds, then on high for about 30 seconds.

Pour wet into dry and fold 2 or 3 times. Gradually add carrots and raisins and continue to fold until just blended.

Pour batter into cake pan and smooth with spatula.

Bake for 48-50 minutes or until slightly browned. Cool in pan on a cooling rack for 10 minutes. Use spatula to loosen from edges. Then flip onto a plate, and then back over again onto a cooling rack, so the top side is again on top. Let cool.

Serve chilled.

Chocolate Fudge Cake

(This is a rich, dense almost fudge-like chocolate 2 layer cake with a slight taste of banana and an occasional chocolate chip. This makes a nice Christmas cake.)

Pre-heat oven to 350°F. Oil two 9" round cake pans.

Dry Ingredients:

2 ¼ c white spelt flour (and 1 Tbsp for pans)   2 Tbsp tapioca starch
1 ¾ c sugar   1 tsp baking soda
1 c cocoa powder (and 1 tsp for pans)   1 ½ tsp xanthan gum
½ c potato starch   1 tsp baking powder
1 ½ tsp soy lecithin powder   1 tsp salt

Wet Ingredients:

1 2/3 c rice milk   1/3 c ripe banana
1 c safflower oil   2 Tbsp water
½ c apple sauce   1 Tbsp vanilla extract

Additional Ingredients:

1/3 c chocolate chips

Flour cake pans with mixture of the Tbsp flour and the tsp cocoa, throwing away excess.

Mix dry ingredients and sift.

Blend wet ingredients in blender on low for 15 seconds and on high for 1 minute.

Pour wet into dry. Mix briefly to partially incorporate the flour.

Mix with electric mixer for 2 minutes, briefly on low and then on high. (If using a hand mixer, note that this is a thick batter, and therefore may be a slight challenge for the hand mixer to handle. If the batter starts rising too high up the beaters, lower speed and then raise beaters slightly out of batter until batter recedes again.)

Pour into cake pans. Cook about 43 minutes, or until springs to the touch, and a toothpick comes out clean.

Easter Egg Cake

You will need:
Yellow Birthday Cake (see page 94)
Creamy White Frosting (see page 121)
Food coloring (or small bits of jam to mix with the frosting)
Coconut (optional, and if allergies allow)

Cut one layer of the cake into Easter egg shape. Place it over other layer of the cake to trace the shape. Cut bottom layer to match top layer. (Or, of course, if you can find two egg shaped pans, you can simply use those.) Divide frosting into 2 or three bowls. Color each bowl of frosting with a different color food coloring. When cake is fully cooled, decorate the cake to look like an Easter egg, making patterns with the different colors. Sprinkle some or all of it with coconut.

Gingerbread

Dry Ingredients:

1 c white spelt flour
½ c whole spelt flour
½ c tapioca flour
2/3 c sugar
1 ½ tsp ginger
1 tsp baking soda
1 tsp soy lecithin powder

1 tsp cream of tartar
½ tsp baking powder
½ tsp xanthan gum
½ tsp salt
¼ tsp cinnamon
¼ tsp cloves

Wet Ingredients:

½ c safflower oil
1/3 c rice milk
1/3 c apple sauce

3 Tbsp molasses*
2 Tbsp water

Optional Ingredient:

½ c raisins

Mix together dry ingredients with fork, and sift 1 time. Set aside. Put wet ingredients into a bowl and stir.

When wet ingredients are at room temperature, pre-heat oven to 350°F. Oil an 8" x 8" pan.

Pour wet into dry, and mix with an electric mixer, first on low briefly and then on medium/high for 2 minutes. If using raisins, add gradually over last 15 seconds of mixing. The batter will be thick and elastic.

Pour into cake pan, and spread evenly. Bake for 35 minutes. Cool in pan. Serve warm with Vanilla Rice Milk Ice Cream (see page 96), or room temperature.

Optional: For a stronger molasses flavor, substitute one Tbsp of the water with an additional one Tbsp molasses, totaling ¼ c molasses.

Gingerbread #2

Pre-heat oven to 350°F. Oil an 8" x 8" pan.

Dry Ingredients:

¾ c sugar

½ c quinoa flour

½ c buckwheat flour (has a bit of gluten)

½ c tapioca flour

¼ c white rice flour

¼ c rice bran

1 ¾ tsp ginger

1 tsp soy lecithin powder

1 tsp baking soda

1 tsp cream of tartar

½ tsp baking powder

½ tsp xanthan gum

½ tsp salt

½ tsp cinnamon

¼ tsp cloves

Wet Ingredients:

½ c safflower oil

½ c rice milk

¼ c apple sauce

3 Tbsp molasses*

Optional Ingredient:

½ c raisins

Mix together dry ingredients with fork, and sift 1 time. Set aside. Put wet ingredients into a bowl and stir.

Pour wet into dry, and mix with an electric mixer, first on low until all is combined, and then on medium/high, for 2 minutes. The batter will be thick and elastic. If using raisins, add them gradually over the last 15 seconds of mixing.

Pour into cake pan, and spread evenly but quickly. Bake for 40-45 minutes, or until springs to the touch. Cool in pan. Serve warm with Vanilla Rice Milk Ice Cream (see page 96), or room temperature.

*Optional: For a stronger molasses flavor, substitute 1 Tbsp of the water with an additional 1 Tbsp molasses, totaling ¼ c molasses.

Glazed Blueberry Cake
(a beautiful cake for summer entertaining)

Pre-heat oven to 350°F. Oil and very lightly flour a 9" x 9" square cake pan.

Dry Ingredients:

3/4 c barley flour
3/4 c oat flour
1 c sugar
1/3 c potato starch
1 Tbsp arrowroot flour (or tapioca flour)

1 tsp lecithin powder
1 tsp baking powder
½ tsp baking soda
½ tsp xanthan gum
¼ tsp salt

Wet Ingredients:

1/3 c rice milk
1/3 c safflower oil
¼ c ripe peeled, chopped Bartlett pear

2 Tbsp lemon juice
1 Tbsp water
1 tsp vanilla extract

Extra Ingredients:

1 c fresh (washed and dried) or frozen blueberries
If blueberries are frozen: 1 tsp barley flour and 1 tsp sugar

Mix dry ingredients and sift 3 times.

If using frozen blueberries, thaw by rinsing with cold water in colander or strainer. Pat reasonably dry, sprinkle with the "extra ingredients" flour/sugar mixture, and stir to coat.

Blend wet ingredients in blender on low for 15 seconds, then on high for 1 minute. Pour wet into dry and fold gently until almost blended. Add blueberries and fold until just blended. Pour and spread batter evenly in cake pan. Bake for 50 minutes or until slightly browned. Cool in pan on a cooling rack for 10 minutes. Use stiff spatula to loosen from edge. Then flip onto a plate, and then back right side up onto cooling rack.

When cool, move onto a serving dish. Drizzle top and a bit on the dish with 1/2 recipe of Fruit (Blueberry) Glaze (see page 124). (The other half recipe is great on fruit, ice cream, or pancakes!)

Lemon Cake
(This casually elegant very lemony cake has a
slightly dry cornbread-like texture from the rice flour.)

Pre-heat oven to 350°F. Oil and lightly flour one 9" round cake pan.

Dry Ingredients:
2/3 c + 2 Tbsp white rice flour 1 tsp baking soda
1/3 c + 2 tsp potato starch ½ tsp xanthan gum
1/3 c tapioca flour ½ tsp salt
2/3 c sugar ½ tsp cream of tartar
1 tsp soy lecithin powder

Wet Ingredients:
1 tsp lightly packed freshly grated lemon peel (peel from about ½ a
lemon)
1/3 c safflower oil 2 Tbsp apple sauce
1/3 c lemon juice 1 Tbsp warm water

Final Ingredient:
1 Tbsp powdered sugar

Mix dry ingredients with fork, and sift 3 times. Set aside.

Put wet ingredients in blender. Blend on low speed for about 15
seconds, then on high for about 15 seconds.

Pour wet into dry and fold gently until just mixed. The batter will
be very light and soft.

Spread in cake pan.

Bake 30 minutes. Place pan on a cooling rack for 5 minutes.
Then remove from pan and let finish cooling on cooling rack.

Put powdered sugar into a sifter. Sprinkle the sugar lightly and
evenly over the top of the cake by sifting it onto the cake.

More ideas:

- Try placing a few berries on and/or around the cake.

- For a slightly fancier cake, make a double recipe for a two layer
cake, and use a thin layer of Fruit (Blueberry) Glaze (see page 124)
between the layers.

Snowman Cake

(This cake is great fun to bring into a child's classroom for a winter holiday party. It will receive lots of "oohs" and "ahs.")

You Will Need:

A very large, completely flat rectangular serving platter, or a large piece of corrugated cardboard to serve the same function. Ideal is about 3 feet by about 16".

Aluminum foil

Wax paper (or plastic wrap)

Two 9" round layers of white colored cake, and two smaller layers (5" or 6")

Creamy white frosting (see page 121)

Chocolate frosting (optional, see page 117)

Chanukah gelt (chocolate coins covered with gold foil)*, about 3 dozen

2 blueberries (or raisins)

1 carrot

1 red apple

Semisweet chocolate chips (about ½ c)

Two honey sticks - clear straws filled with honey and sealed (or anything else that will make good snowman arms)

Completely cover serving platter or cardboard with aluminum foil, shiny side showing.

Line the edges of the platter with wax paper (later to be removed along with excess frosting)

Place one of the large cake layers about 3 inches from one of the short ends of the tray. This will be the base of the snowman. The outer ½" to 1" of the sides and bottom (but not the top) of the cake layer should be resting on the wax paper. If not, add more wax paper. Frost this piece with white frosting.

To make the middle section of the snowman fit snugly on the base, cut a small slightly rounded piece off what will be the lower end of the second round cake, matching the shape of the top of the base. Build the snowman by fitting this piece on the tray just over the base. Frost this piece with white frosting.

Repeat this procedure with one of the small cake layers to make the head, this time cutting out an even smaller portion of cake. Fit it onto the center portion. Then slice off the top inch or so in a straight line, making a place for the hat to fit. Again, frost with white frosting.

Now for the hat. Take the final small layer. Cut off the bottom in a straight line, but this time start the cut much higher up so that you are removing 1/4 to 1/3 of the layer. Then shape the sides of the hat by removing two more pieces: First, cut out a bit from about 1:00 to 3:00, leaving an "L" shaped right side of the hat. Then do a similar cut from 9:00 to 11:00 to leave a backwards "L' shaped left side of the hat. Frost the straight edge of the hat with chocolate (or white) frosting, and place hat against top of the head section.

Frost the rest of the hat. Cover the frosting with chocolate chips, and then gently press the chips (saving a few) down into the frosting so they stay firmly attached.

Make the eyes with the blueberries, the nose with a small piece from the end of the carrot, the mouth by cutting a smile shaped wedge off the apple, and buttons with chocolate chips. (Or use whatever foods you would enjoy.)

Slide the wax paper out from under the cake, leaving clean foil beneath.

Add the honey stick arms.

When ready to serve, use most of the chocolate coins to make a "ground" under the snowman. Spread a few elsewhere around the tray, like glistening snowflakes. Then, enjoy displaying your creation!

You may want to use enough coins to be able to serve a chocolate coin along with each slice of cake.

*Vermont Nut Free at www.Vermontnutfree.com sells these during the winter holiday season. They state that their semisweet chocolate is peanut and tree nut free, but that it could have traces of dairy.

Strawberry Shortcake
(makes 12 servings)

Every year my town has a huge Strawberry Festival in June. Central to the festival is strawberry shortcake. My family had always steered clear of the shortcake area, so that my son wouldn't have to watch people eat such a delicious treat that he couldn't have too. Then one year I realized there was another option! I could bake some shortcake for the festival that my son and other people with food allergies *would* be able to eat!

It didn't take much work. In case you have a similar opportunity, here were the steps:

Ask the shortcake committee if they would be interested in serving this if I provided it.

Suggest to the committee that they mention it in Strawberry Festival related newspaper articles, so that parents of kids with allergies would know that they could bring their kids to the shortcake area.

Make a sign for the stand: "Shortcake for people with food allergies is available! Please ask."

Make two ingredient lists – one to put near those those taking money for the shortcake, and one for the shortcake serving area.

Since at the time I didn't have a commercial kitchen, the committee decided to draw up a consent form for parents to sign saying that the parents took responsibility for their choice to try my shortcake.

The morning of the Festival, I received a call from two parents asking if I would please reserve shortcake for their children, in case we would be running out before they arrived. Those simple requests made the effort more than worth it. And the best part was still to come: watching my son and other people with food allergies thoroughly enjoying strawberry shortcake with everyone else.

Dry Ingredients:
1 c white rice flour
2/3 c sugar
½ c + 1 ½ tsp potato starch
¼ c tapioca flour
1 tsp baking soda
1 tsp soy lecithin powder
½ tsp xanthan gum
½ tsp salt
½ tsp cream of tartar
¼ tsp baking powder

Wet Ingredients:
1/3 c rice milk
1/3 c safflower oil
1 Tbsp vanilla extract
1 Tbsp apple sauce
2 tsp lemon juice

Preheat oven to 425°F.

Oil 1 muffin pan.

Mix dry ingredients thoroughly with fork, then sift 3 times. Set aside.

Put wet ingredients in blender. Blend on low speed for 15 seconds and then on high speed for 1 minute.

Pour wet into dry, and fold gently until just mixed.

Spoon batter portions into muffin pan. Bake 13 minutes at 425°F. Transfer to cookie rack to cool. Serve whole, or slice the top off the bottom with a serrated knife, and serve both sides open side up (like an English muffin) in a bowl, covered with strawberry sauce, or with whatever topping works for you. Note: If your shortbread will be outside in the heat prior to serving, try to keep the container open to the air to maintain a good consistency.

Serve with Strawberry Sauce (see page 124).

Valentine's Day Cake

Follow recipe for Vanilla Pear Cake and Cupcakes (see page 93) (or other cake), and Creamy White Frosting (see page 121) and do any one or combination of the following options:

-Bake the cake in a heart shaped pan.
-Use a regular round pan but then cut the cake down to a heart shape, and frost to cover the cut edges.
-Cut each of two layers into heart shapes, with the top heart smaller than the bottom heart.
-Decorate cake or cupcakes with heart shaped candy.
-Color the frosting pink.
-Place an open-top heart shaped cookie cutter on the cake. Pour colorful sprinkles over the frosting inside the cookie cutter. Press the sprinkles down a bit into the frosting. Remove the cookie cutter. There will be a heart made of sprinkles. Repeat if desired.
-Similarly, cut hearts out of waxed paper (by folding the paper and cutting half heart shapes). Then lay the waxed paper gently over the frosted cake and fill heart holes with sprinkes. Press down gently, and remove paper.
-Make white frosting and set some aside. Use the rest of the frosting to frost the cake. Color the extra frosting pink/red. Use a pointy knife to outline a heart shape in the frosted cake. Carefully fill in the heart with the colored frosting.

Vanilla Cake with Blueberry Peach Sauce
(This is a beautiful cake for entertaining!)

Prepare one layer of Vanilla Pear Cake (see page 93).

Let cool to room temperature, and place on a serving dish (12"-14" round).

Scoop out a very shallow bowl (instant sampling!) from the middle 5" of the top of the cake, being careful not to poke a hole through the bottom.

Prepare Vanilla Fudge Frosting (see page 122).

Lightly frost the top (not the sides) of the cake with frosting. Let that cool and harden.

Make Blueberry Peach Sauce (see page 122). Let cool until warm but not hot. (Transferring the sauce out of the pan into a dish, and then into a different dish, will help hasten the cooling process.) Spoon each peach slice (with a little sauce and blueberries) into the middle of the cake, filling the "bowl". Set each slice down next to the one before it so that the peaches form a flower shape – each piece extending from the very middle of the cake out toward the outside, forming a circle. When all the peaches are out of the sauce dish, pour the rest of the sauce on the rest of the top of the cake, especially around the top edge, allowing sauce to drip over the edge to coat the sides of the cake. Gently prod any blueberries that are not in the "bowl" section of the cake top over the edge of the cake onto the plate. These will form a saucy section ½ inch to an inch wide around the edge of the cake on the serving dish.

Refrigerate for an hour or longer, and serve!

Alternate recipe: If you are able to put this cake together right before serving, you might choose to skip the frosting layer all together. The frosting layer provides a nice contrast of a very sweet almost crunchy middle, and keeps the fruit sauce from seeping into the top of the cake. Delicious as that is, a lighter, less sweet, and potentially warm version would be to pour the sauce directly on the cake right before serving.

Frostings and Sauces

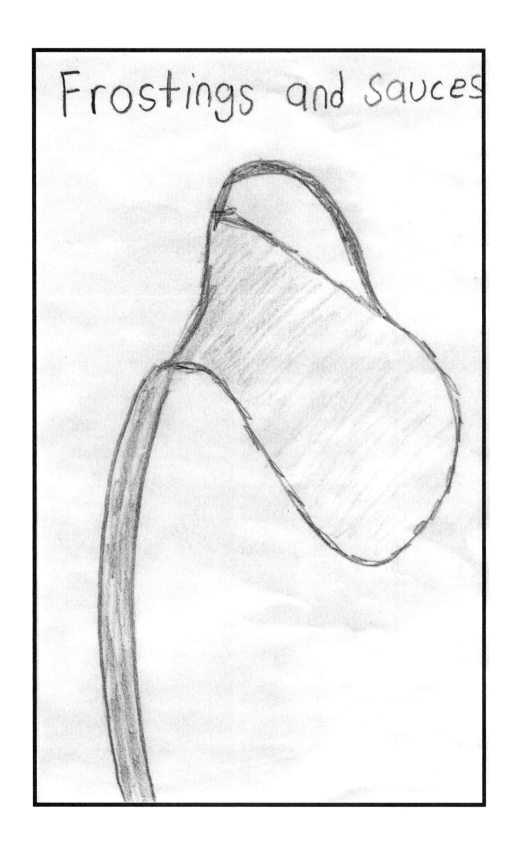

Chocolate Sauces and Frostings

Here you will find several chocolate sauces and frostings. Each gets thicker and richer than the one before.

Chocolate Frosting is a sweet frosting that is similar to "regular" frostings, in that it is made predominantly from confectioner sugar.
Chocolate Sauce is a liquid Chocolate Sauce that can be stored in the refrigerator. It is good drizzled over Rice Cream Ice Cream, cakes, or even pancakes. It's also great for chocolate (rice) milk or hot chocolate.
Hot Fudge is made from actual chocolate, rather than cocoa, so it is thick and rich. It works great as a hot sauce. Unlike Chocolate Sauce, it will congeal into a frosting when cooled. It is then called **Fudge Frosting**. This is less sweet than Chocolate Frosting, and has a creamier consistency.
Chocolate Spread is very thick and rich, almost like fudge. Try between cookies, or as the frosting in the middle of a vanilla cake.

Chocolate Frosting
(plenty for a two layer cake with extra to spare)

Ingredients:
¾ c safflower oil
1/3 c rice milk
2 tsp vanilla extract
½ tsp soy lecithin powder
¼ tsp cream of tartar
1 ½ c chocolate chips
3 c powdered sugar

If the powdered sugar is at all lumpy, sift it prior to mixing it with the other ingredients. Put all ingredients into a large pan. Turn heat on low. Stir steadily until blended, melted, and smooth, like a slightly thick chocolate soup. Pour into a bowl, to facilitate rapid cooling. When still warm but no longer hot, spread onto cake. It will pour and spread easily. As it cools to room temperature, it will become the firmness of frosting.

Chocolate Sauce

Ingredients:
½ c cocoa powder
½ c rice milk
¼ c rice syrup (or maple syrup)
2 Tbsp maple syrup
2 tsp vanilla extract
½ tsp soy lecithin powder
¼ tsp xanthan gum

Combine ingredients. Beat with whisk or fork until smooth.

Hot Fudge/Fudge Frosting

Ingredients:
1 c chocolate chips
1/3 c rice milk
¼ tsp soy lecithin powder
¼ tsp xanthan gum
2 Tbsp rice syrup (or maple syrup)
1 Tbsp maple syrup
2 tsp vanilla extract
2 Tbsp powdered sugar

Melt chips in milk on double boiler on medium heat (water not boiling). Stir until smooth. Add remaining ingredients in the order listed, stirring between each one. At end, stir well. Serve warm as a rich chocolate sauce. Or, let cool to slightly warm and spread on cake as frosting.

Chocolate Spread
(for a single layer)

Ingredients:
1 c chocolate chips
2 Tbsp (or a few more drops if needed) rice milk
½ c powdered sugar
2 tsp vanilla extract

Melt chips in milk on double boiler on medium heat (water not boiling). Stir. Add vanilla. Stir. Add powdered sugar. Stir well. If too thick, add a teaspoon or two more rice milk. When fully blended, allow to cool almost to room temperature. Spread on cake.

Gingerbread Frosting
(Use to decorate gingerbread people, p. 73.)

Ingredients:
½ c powdered sugar
2 tsp warm rice milk
¼ tsp vanilla extract
1/8 tsp cream of tartar

Mix well.
If too dry, add more rice milk, a ½ tsp at a time.

Lemon Icing and Frosting

Dry Ingredients:
2 1/3 c powdered sugar for icing; 3 c for frosting
½ tsp cream of tartar
1 pinch of salt

Wet Ingredients:
¼ c hot water
2 ½ tsp lemon juice
½ tsp vanilla extract

Mix and then sift the powdered sugar with the salt and cream of tartar. Mix the remaining ingredients in a small bowl. Add them to the dry mixture. Whisk with a fork until smooth.

Maple Frosting

Dry Ingredients:
4 ½ c powdered sugar
½ tsp cream of tartar
1 pinch of salt

Wet Ingredients:
1/3 c very hot water
2 Tbsp maple syrup for a mildly maple flavor, or 3 Tbsp for a stronger maple flavor

Mix and then sift the powdered sugar with the salt and cream of tartar. Mix the remaining ingredients in a small bowl. Add them gradually to the dry mixture while stirring. Mix on low speed for a few seconds, then on medium speed for 2 minutes or until very creamy and smooth.

Orange Frosting
(a light, thin, creamy frosting)

Dry Ingredients:
2 c powdered sugar
½ tsp cream of tartar
1 pinch of salt

Wet Ingredients:
2 Tbsp frozen orange juice concentrate, thawed
2 Tbsp boiling water

Mix and then sift the powdered sugar with the salt and cream of tartar. Mix the orange juice concentrate with the water in a small bowl. Add them to the dry mixture. Blend with spatula. Mix on low speed with an electric mixer for a few seconds, then on medium speed for 2 minutes.

Creamy White Frosting

Dry Ingredients:
2 ¼ - 3 c̊ powdered sugar
1 tsp cream of tartar
1 pinch of salt

Wet Ingredients:
1 c canola oil chilled

Mix 2 ¼ c powdered sugar with the salt and cream of tartar, and sift one time.

Add the oil to the dry mixture. Blend with spatula.

Mix with an electric mixer on low speed for a few seconds, then on medium speed. During mixing, add more sifted sugar to desired thickness. More sugar will make a thicker frosting. Total mixing should be about 2 minutes, or slightly longer if adding more sugar.

Vanilla Icing and Frosting

Dry Ingredients:
2 ½ c powdered sugar for icing, 3 c for frosting
1 pinch salt
¼ tsp cream of tartar

Wet Ingredients:
1 Tbsp rice milk
2 Tbsp water

1 tsp lemon juice
1 Tbsp vanilla extract

Mix and then sift the dry ingredients.

Place the wet ingredients except for the vanilla extract into a small pot. Heat until close to boiling. Remove from heat, add the vanilla extract, and stir.

Add wet ingredients to dry ingredients.

Whisk with fork until smooth.

Vanilla Fudge Frosting

Use recipe for Creamy White Frosting (see page 122), but before it is close to boiling do the following: Mix 1 tsp water with 1 tsp arrowroot powder. Add to pot and simmer for 1 minute, stirring throughout. Then proceed with recipe. Let cool for a couple of minutes. Then drizzle over baked item, and immediately spread with spatula – before it starts to cool and harden.

Fruit Icing and Frosting

Follow recipe for Vanilla Icing and Frosting (see page 121), but use an additional 1 Tbsp powdered sugar and add 2 tsp fruit jam. Apricot, strawberry, and raspberry work well. This provides great natural food coloring and flavor.

Blueberry Peach Sauce

Fruit Ingredients:

10 oz. bag of frozen blueberries	1/ 4 c apple juice
10 oz. bag of frozen peach slices	1 tsp lemon juice
1 c sugar	

Final Ingredients:

1 1/ 2 tsp arrowroot powder	1 tsp cold water

Put the frozen fruit in a colander or strainer and run cold water over it to rinse off any ice crystals.

Put Fruit Ingredients into a pan and cook for 15 minutes on medium heat, stirring frequently, with the mixture bubbling gently.

Combine the arrowroot powder and the cold water, and stir until smooth. Add to pan, and continue cooking for 5 more minutes.

Cherry (or other fruit) Syrup

Dry Ingredients:
¼ c brown sugar, tightly packed
¼ c turbinado (or white) sugar

Wet Ingredients:
2 Tbsp canola oil
1 Tbsp honey
1 Tbsp cherry (or other) juice (or, for an adult gathering, try cherry liqueur!)

Additional Ingredient:
2 Tbsp pitted, chopped fresh or frozen cherries (or other fruit)*
1 ½ tsp arrowroot powder
1 tsp cold water

Mix dry ingredients, breaking up any clumps.

Put wet ingredients into a small pot and mix.

Add dry ingredients and mix.

Heat on low, stirring frequently until smooth (about 1 minute).

Mix the arrowroot with the water until smooth. Add to pot and stir for about 1 minute.

Add cherries. Continue to heat on low, stirring frequently, for about 5 more minutes.

Strain into something that will later be easy to pour from, such as a glass measuring cup, pressing on the cherry pieces with the back of a spoon to get as much as possible through the strainer. Throw away the cherry pieces that are still caught in the strainer. If not using right away, cover the mixture (so that the top doesn't congeal.) Let cool briefly to thicken.

*   Raspberry Syrup: Substitute raspberries for the cherries.
Blueberry Syrup: Substitute blueberries for the cherries.
Strawberry Syrup: Substitute strawberries for the cherries.

Fruit Glaze
(cherry, blueberry, strawberry, or raspberry)

Follow recipe for Cherry (or other fruit) Syrup (see page 123), but increase the arrowroot powder to 2 ½ tsp. For the blueberry glaze, substitute pear juice for the apple juice.

Cover the mixture (so that the top doesn't congeal.) Let cool to slightly warm (about 30 minutes). The mixture will be thicker but still easy to pour.

Spread or drizzle over a cake, or use between layers of a cake.

Strawberry Sauce

Fruit Ingredients:
4 c fresh sliced strawberries (or 2 10 oz. bags of frozen strawberries)
1 c sugar
¼ c apple juice
1 tsp lemon juice

Final Ingredients:
1 tsp arrowroot powder
1 tsp cold water

If using frozen strawberries, put them in a colander or strainer and run cold water over them to rinse off any ice crystals.

Put Fruit Ingredients into a pan and cook for 15 minutes on medium heat, stirring frequently, with the mixture bubbling gently.

Combine the arrowroot powder and the cold water, and stir until smooth. Add to pan, and continue cooking for 5 more minutes.

Serve over Strawberry Shortcake (see page 111), pancakes, waffles, or (r)ice cream.

Crisps, Cobbler, Pudding, and Pies

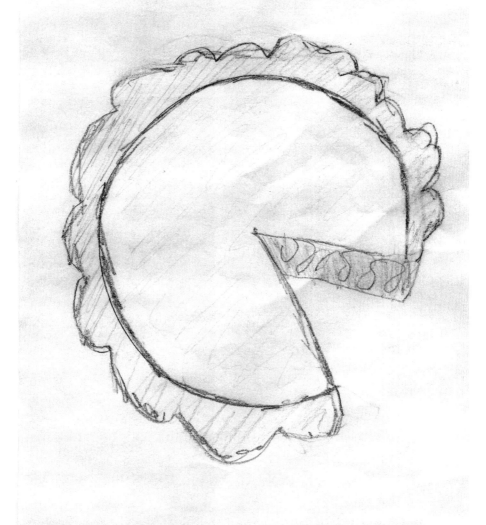

Apple Crisp (and peach crisp)
(a sweet dessert)

Crisp Topping Dry Ingredients:
1 ¾ c old fashioned rolled oats
¼ c oat flour
¾ c brown sugar
1 ½ tsp cinnamon
¼ tsp ground ginger

Crisp Topping Wet Ingredients:
1/3 c canola oil
1 tsp vanilla extract

Apple Ingredients:
6 c sliced, peeled apples* (about 5 large Granny Smith or Cortland apples)
1 c sugar
1 Tbsp honey
1 Tbsp cinnamon
½ tsp salt

Thickening Ingredients:
5 tsp arrowroot flour
1 Tbsp cold water

Start by making the Crisp Topping: Mix dry ingredients, mix wet ingredients, pour wet into dry, and mix.

Oil a 9" x 9" cake pan. Preheat oven to 400°F.

Put "apple ingredients" in a pan. Heat on medium/low, gently stirring occasionally, until the sugar has dissolved and the mixture (except for the fruit) has become smooth (about 2 minutes). Although it will be dry initially, it will get wet as it heats.

Mix the arrowroot with the water and stir until smooth. Pour into the pan, and stir. Cook for 4-5 minutes, stirring frequently.

Use a slotted spoon to scoop the fruit out of the pan into the oiled baking dish, leaving most of the sauce behind. (Do NOT discard.)

Spread the fruit evenly.

Drizzle 1 Tbsp of the sauce over it.

Spread Crisp Topping over the mixture.

Drizzle ¼ c of the sauce over the topping.

Bake for 20 minutes.

Serve warm. Try with Rice Milk Ice Cream (see page 96).

*Peach crisp alternative: Substitute peaches for the apples to make peach crisp. Adjust the fruit mixture by reducing the cinnamon to 1 ½ tsp, and increasing the sugar to 1 ¼ c. In pan, reduce the 4-5 minutes to 2-3 minutes. Try with Peach (R)ice Cream (see page 97).

Peach Cobbler

Oil a 9" x 9" cake pan.
Preheat oven to 400°F.

Peach Filling
Ingredients:
4 c fresh (or frozen) peeled and sliced peaches (If frozen, two 10 oz packages)

1 1/8 c (1 c plus 2 Tbsp) sugar   1 ½ tsp cinnamon

¼ c honey   ½ tsp salt

Thickening Ingredients:
1/3 c barley flour   1 Tbsp arrowroot flour

2 tsp cold water

Additional Ingredient:
1 Tbsp sugar

Pastry Ingredients:
Dry Ingredients:
1 1/8 c (1 c plus 2 Tbsp) barley flour   1 tsp baking powder

½ c oat flour   1 tsp cream of tartar

¾ c sugar   ½ tsp xanthan gum

3 Tbsp tapioca starch   ¼ tsp salt

1 tsp soy lecithin powder

Wet Ingredients:
½ c rice milk   1 tsp lemon juice

1/3 c canola oil

1 Tbsp fresh, frozen (thawed and room temperature), or canned peaches

Final Ingredient:
1 Tbsp sugar

Prepare fruit. If using frozen fruit, put it into a bowl to thaw.

Mix "pastry" dry ingredients together in a bowl and sift one time. Set aside.

Put wet ingredients in blender to finish warming to room temperature.

Put "peach filling ingredients" in a pan. Heat on medium/low, gently stirring occasionally, until the sugar has dissolved and the mixture (except for the peaches) has become smooth (about a minute). Although it will be dry initially, it will get wet as the sweeteners melt and the fruit cooks.

Next come the "thickening ingredients": Mix the arrowroot with the water and stir until smooth. Pour into the pan, and stir. Then add the flour. Cook for 2-3 minutes, frequently stirring.

Pour into oiled pan, spreading the peaches evenly.

Sprinkle top of filling with the "additional ingredient" sugar. Bake for 8 minutes.

When fruit is about to come out, blend wet ingredients in blender for 15 seconds on low and one minute on high.

Pour wet into dry and fold gently until barely mixed - occasional specks of flour will still be visible.

Using small amounts at a time, spoon mixture over peaches, trying to drop a little bit over each spot as best as possible, with particular attention to the edges. Then use a spatula to smooth out the batter to fully cover fruit, being gentle so that the peach arrangement does not move. This will be a very thin layer.

Sprinkle top with last Tbsp of sugar.

Bake for 30 minutes until top has browned.

Serve warm. Try with Rice Milk Ice Cream (see page 96). For a super peachy treat, serve it with Peach Rice Milk Ice Cream (see page 97).

Upside-Down Pear Gingerbread

Oil 9" x 9" cake pan. Pre-heat oven to 325°F.

Dry Ingredients:

1 1/3 c white rice flour

½ c sorghum flour

½ c potato starch

¼ c sugar

2 Tbsp tapioca flour

4 tsp ground ginger

2 tsp cinnamon

1 ½ tsp lecithin powder

1 tsp xanthan gum

1 tsp baking powder

1 tsp baking soda

½ tsp salt

¼ tsp nutmeg

¼ tsp cloves

Wet Ingredients:

1/3 c safflower oil

¾ c rice milk

2/3 c Bosc (or Bartlett) pears (about 1 pear), peeled and sliced

¼ c dark molasses (Hint: Dip measuring cup into oil mixture before filling with molasses, and the molasses will slide out easily.)

½ c brown sugar

Pear Ingredients:

3 Tbsp safflower oil

¼ c brown sugar

¼ c sugar

1 tsp arrowroot powder

4 Bosc pears (3 if very large)

Mix dry ingredients together and sift 3 times.

Put wet ingredients into blender.

Prepare pear mixture: Measure the sugars and set aside. Peel, core, and quarter each pear. Slice each quarter lengthwise into 3 (or 4, if the quarter is very large) long slices. Heat the oil in a pan on medium/low. Add the sugars and stir until mixed. (The oil will be completely absorbed.) Add the pears, and simmer for 5 minutes, stirring steadily until the sugars are melted and the pears are coated, and then occasionally after that. Turn heat to very low. Sprinkle arrowroot powder over pears and stir well.

Pour into cake pan, spreading pears evenly.

Blend the wet ingredients on low speed for 15 seconds, then on high speed for 1 minute.

Pour wet into dry, and fold gently until just mixed. Pour thin layer over pears, trying to cover all spots, especially the edges. Use spatula to fill in any holes, and to gently even the surface of the batter if needed.

Cook for 55 minutes, until springs to the touch. Let cool 5 minutes in pan, on a rack. Loosen edges gently with spatula. Then put serving pan on top of cake pan like a cover, put hand over middle of serving dish, and flip both dishes over so that cake falls out onto serving dish. Serve warm.

Rice Pudding
(great for using up leftover rice!)

Ingredients:
1/3 c rice milk
2/3 c peeled, chopped apple
1 ½ c cooked rice (short grain brown rice, or any other) tightly packed
¼ c raisins
¼ c grade A dark maple syrup
2 Tbsp apple juice
1 tsp arrowroot powder
2 tsp tapioca starch
¼ tsp salt
1 tsp vanilla extract
½ tsp cinnamon
¼ tsp xanthan gum
½ tsp additional cinnamon
1 tsp sugar

Pre-heat oven to 375°F.

Oil a medium size (1 to 1 ½ quarts, which is the same as 4 to 6 cups) shallow round baking dish – a clear Pyrex dish is especially nice because it will enable you to see the pudding.

Mix together the last two ingredients (cinnamon and sugar). Set aside.

Put all remaining ingredients into a pot. Stir. Cook on a low heat, covered, for 5 minutes, stirring occasionally.

Spread the mixture evenly into the bowl.

Sprinkle the cinnamon sugar mixture over the top of the mixture.

Bake for 20 minutes.

Let sit for at least 10 minutes prior to serving, to allow some setting to take place. Can be enjoyed warm, room temperature, or cold.

Try with a dollop of (r)ice cream on top (see page 96).

Oatmeal Pie Crust

This crust makes enough to cover the bottom and top of a small pie (8 ½" and shallow), or to cover the bottom and sprinkle the top of a large one (10" and deep).

Follow recipe for the alternate version of Cranberry Oatmeal Cookies (see page 69) except:
Leave out the baking powder and the cranberries.
After chilling the batter:
Put dough into pie pan: Use about 1 cup of the dough for a small pie, and about 1 1/3 c for a large one. Cover loosely with plastic wrap. Over the plastic wrap and using a (straight) water glass, roll the dough across the bottom and against the sides of the pan. Remove the wrap and use fingers or a fork to finish pressing dough into edges and up sides as needed.
Fill with pie filling. If making a top, use a fork to drop bits of dough over the top of the pie until covered. Bake as directed for the pie.

[choice of flour]

Super Quick Pie Crust

For each 4" X 4" section of dish you wish to cover, crush into crumbs 1/3 cup of your favorite cold cereal or cookies (or, for those not allergic to wheat, 2 graham crackers), and mix with 2 Tbsp canola oil. For a full pie crust, then, try 1 1/3 cups of crumble mixed with ½ cup oil. Spread onto bottom of dish and a bit up the sides. Add pie mixture and bake according to pie instructions.

Pie Crust
(double crust)

Unlike cake ingredients, pie crust ingredients need to be cold.

Dry Ingredients:

1 ¾ c white spelt	½ tsp salt
½ c whole spelt	2 Tbsp sugar
1/3 c oat flour	¼ tsp cinnamon
1 Tbsp white rice flour	

Wet Ingredients:

3/4 c safflower oil (cold)	¼ c apple juice

Combine wet ingredients in a cup and put in freezer for 15 – 20 minutes to further chill.

Mix dry ingredients thoroughly with a fork, sift one time, and refrigerate until the frozen ingredients are ready.

If needing a pre-baked crust, preheat oven to 400°F.

Add the chilled liquids and blend quickly with a fork just until there is no loose flour. At this point and throughout preparation, handle dough as little as possible for a tender crust.

Divide dough in two, and form each of the two sections into a ball. Wrap one in plastic wrap, put it in a bowl, and refrigerate it (overnight if possible).

Rip 2 pieces of wax paper (or parchment paper), each piece about 3 feet long. Fold each in half, and set one aside for when you later roll the top dough.

Open the remaining piece of wax paper. Place the remaining dough in the middle of one side of the wax paper, flatten it a bit with your hands, and then close the wax paper over it. The dough should now rest in the middle of the folded wax paper, with paper beneath and above it.

Roll the dough out by using a rolling pin over the top of the wax paper. Always start each stroke from the center of the dough, and roll outwards, alternating direction with each stroke. Use even pressure except at the edges, where slightly lightening the pressure prevents the edges from getting too thin.

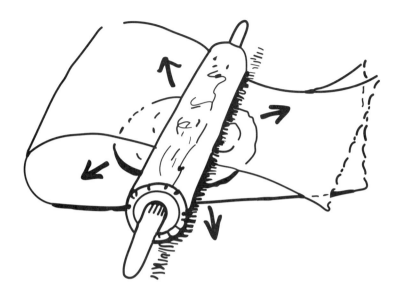

When the dough is wide enough to cover the bottom and sides of the pie pan, gently peel the top paper off the dough; as needed, use your fingers to help push the dough off the paper. When the paper is fully loose, set it loosely back over the dough. Then flip over the whole paper/dough "sandwich", so that the bottom paper becomes the top one. Repeat the peeling procedure to loosen it, too.

Open the paper again, and gently place the pie pan, upside down, onto the dough. Flip the pan and dough so that the dough settles into the pan. Remove paper, helping dough settle more into place. Trim excess dough. Save it in case it is needed for the top dough to fill in any holes – if not, perhaps someone will want to play with it!

If baking the crust empty, make a few pricks with a fork or steak knife before cooking to help prevent bubbles forming, and then bake at 400°F for 15 minutes. Let cool before filling.

Roll out and loosen the top dough just like the first.

Pour the filling into the bottom crust.

Then, take the top dough, and with the wax paper open, and using your hand to support underneath the wax paper, flip the dough over onto the pie. Peel off the paper, trim the dough, and bake.

Apple Pie

1 10" pie pan

Ingredients:
About 9 apples (enough to make 8 c peeled and sliced apples) Try mixing 2 or 3 apple varieties, such as Granny Smith and McIntosh

¾ c sugar	1 tsp canola oil
1 Tbsp oat flour (or potato starch)	2 Tbsp honey
2 Tbsp arrowroot flour (or tapioca flour)	1 Tbsp lemon juice
1 ½ tsp cinnamon	½ c raisins (optional)

Prepare Pie Crust (see page 134, or use alternate crust), refrigerating the bottom dough before rolling it. If you are too short on time to do so, then reduce the cooking time of the bottom crust to 13 minutes. In either case, refrigerate the second ball of dough to be used later for the top crust. Bake bottom crust and let cool.

Blend the sugar, oat flour, arrowroot flour, and cinnamon with a fork, and set aside.

Wash, peel, and slice apples, with each quarter apple sliced into 3 sections. Put into a very large bowl or pot, so there is plenty of room for mixing later.

Roll top crust and set aside.

Put the teaspoon of oil into a tablespoon measuring spoon, swirl around to oil the spoon (so honey won't stick), and then pour the oil into a very small cup or bowl (1/4 c or slightly larger). Measure honey in the oiled tablespoon, and add it to the oil. Add the lemon juice. Stir the oil, honey, and lemon juice with a fork.

Drizzle wet mixture over apples while folding gently.

Sprinkle with the dry flour/sugar mixture while continuing to fold, coating the apples. Pour apples into baked pie crust.

Set top crust in place on pie, and crimp edges.

Bake at 400°F for 30 minutes and then at 375°F for 30 minutes.

Blueberry Pie
(delicious warm as a crumble or chilled as a pie)

1 10" pie pan
2 unbaked pie crusts (see page 134 for Pie Crust, or use alternate)
Preheat oven to 425°F.

Ingredients:
1/3 c honey
¼ c maple syrup
3 Tbsp tapioca flour
½ tsp salt
5 c fresh (or frozen) blueberries
2 tsp lemon juice
2 Tbsp white spelt flour (or barley flour)

Additional Ingredient:
1 Tbsp sugar

Put in a pan the honey, maple syrup, tapioca flour, salt, and 1 cup of the blueberries. Heat on low, stirring occasionally, until the tapioca has dissolved and the mixture has become smooth (except for the blueberries).

Add the lemon juice and flour and stir gently and occasionally until again smooth and gently bubbling. Add the rest of the blueberries and turn off heat. Stir gently until mixed.

Pour into pie crust. Sprinkle top of filling with the sugar.

If desired, cut a shape out of the top crust with a cookie cutter. Place top crust onto pie, and peel the waxed paper off it. If your top crust doesn't have a shape cut out of it, cut a few slits with a knife to allow steam to escape. If you did cut out a shape, you might try "outlining" the shape with thinly rolled strands of extra crust dough.

Pinch bottom and top dough together all the way around (so that the filling won't seep out the sides).

Bake at 425°F for 10 minutes, and then turn heat down to 350°F for 30 minutes.

Cherry Pie

1 8 ½" shallow pie dish
Dough for Oatmeal Pie Crust (see page 133)
Preheat oven to 400°F.

Ingredients:
2 c fresh (or frozen) pitted cherries
2 Tbsp maple syrup
2 Tbsp turbinado (or white) sugar
1 Tbsp honey
1 Tbsp tapioca starch
¼ tsp salt
1 Tbsp oat flour (or white spelt or other flour)
1 tsp lemon juice

Additional Ingredient:
1 Tbsp turbinado (or white) sugar

Roll 1 c of the Oatmeal Pie Crust dough into the pie pan, as directed in that recipe. Set aside the remaining dough.

Put in a pan the honey, sugar, maple syrup, tapioca starch, salt, and ½ cup of the cherries.

Heat on low for about a minute, stirring regularly.

Add the flour and lemon juice, and continue to stir until the mixture is smooth and gently bubbling.

Add the rest of the cherries and turn off heat. Stir until mixed.

Pour into pie crust and spread evenly.

Sprinkle top of filling with the "additional" sugar.

One small forkful at a time, drop bits of the remaining crust dough around the edge and over the top of the pie. When the dough is used up, the cherries (for the most part) will be covered.

Bake at 400°F for 10 minutes, and then turn heat down to 350°F for about 25 minutes or until nicely browned.

Let cool for at least 15 minutes before serving. (It will still be warm, but firmed up a little.) Serve warm or chilled.

Pumpkin Pie

1 9" pie pan
1 unbaked pie crust (see page 134 or alternative)
Preheat oven to 425°F.

Wet Ingredients:
2 15 oz. cans pumpkin puree (3 ½ c) ¾ c maple syrup
½ c unsweetened applesauce 2 tsp vanilla extract

Dry Ingredients:
2 tsp cinnamon ¼ tsp cloves
1 tsp salt ¼ tsp nutmeg
¼ tsp ginger

Other Ingredients:
2 Tbsp agar agar seaweed gel flakes
1 c rice milk

Mix wet ingredients to blend.
Mix dry ingredients with a fork.
Add dry to wet and mix.
Blend mixture in blender a bit at a time until a smooth puree.
Put rice milk in pan. Add agar flakes. Bring to boil. Reduce to simmer for 5 minutes or until agar is essentially dissolved, stirring regularly. Add blender ingredients to pan and stir until evenly blended. If there are lumps, repeat blender process.
Pour into pie crust.
Bake at 425°F for 10 minutes, and then turn down to 350°F for 50-55 minutes. The crust will be lightly browned.
Let cool on a cookie rack until mildly warm (half an hour to an hour). Refrigerate until well chilled to gel the pie. Serve cold.

Fun idea: For a single crusted pumpkin pie at Thanksgiving, re-roll excess crust and use it to make a turkey shape with a turkey cookie cutter. Place this on top of the pie.

Quick Pumpkin Pie

Ingredients:

1 unbaked spelt pie crust (see page 132) or Super Quick Graham Cracker Pie Crust (see page 134) in medium or large pie pan*
1/3 c apple juice
1 c rice milk
4 tsp agar agar seaweed gel flakes
½ c unsweetened applesauce
2 15 oz. cans pumpkin pie mix

Preheat oven to 425°F.

Put apple juice and rice milk into a large pan. Add agar flakes. Bring to boil. Reduce to simmer and stir regularly until agar is dissolved, or for 5 minutes.

Add apple sauce, and stir until again simmering, making sure that any agar from the bottom of pan gets mixed in well.

Add pumpkin and stir over low heat until batter is even throughout – 1 to 2 minutes. It will look like a very thick soup.

Pour into pie crust.

Bake at 425°F for 10 minutes, and then turn down to 350°F for 50-55 minutes. The crust will be lightly browned. Serve chilled.

Note: If your child is going to want to try the pie before it is time to serve it, here's a way to say "Yes!" It is simple to make a side portion for just such a situation. Just use a slightly smaller (but still standard size) pie pan. A 9" pan that is not especially deep will allow you to have just the extra batter you need, while still having a beautiful and full primary pie. Fill the crust to the height you would like your pie to be - the batter will not rise. Then take a small baking dish that seems just the right size for your leftovers. A 4" by 4" pyrex dish is likely to be about right. For that size dish, make one recipe of "Super Quick Crust." Line bottom of dish and a bit up the sides with the crust mixture. Spoon in pumpkin. Bake for 10 minutes less than the pie. Let cool, refrigerate, and serve cold.

*We hope you are enjoying
baking, eating, and sharing these treats.*

*Questions? Comments?
Wonderful stories of people loving what you baked?*

*We love hearing from people,
so feel free to be in touch!*

Gak's Snacks Contact Information

To contact us by mail:
Gak's Snacks, LLC
P.O. Box 491
Windham, NH 03087-0491

To visit our web site and web store, where we offer our own
packaged cookies, coffee cakes, and ingredients:

www.gakssnacks.com

Quantity Conversion Chart

When doubling or halving recipes, it may come in handy to know:
1/3 tablespoon (Tbsp) = 1 teaspoon (tsp)
2/3 Tbsp = 2 tsp
1 Tbsp = 3 tsp
1/8 cup = 2 Tbsp
1/4 cup = 4 Tbsp
1/3 cup = 5 1/3 Tbsp

Original Recipe		1/2 Recipe	
In Cups	In Tablespoons	In Cups	In Tablespoons
1/8	2	1/16	1
1/4	4	1/8	2
1/3	5 1/3	1/6	2 2/3
1/2	8	1/4	4
2/3	10 2/3	1/3	5 1/3
3/4	12	3/8	6
1	16	1/2	8

Original Recipe		Twice Recipe	
In Cups	In Tablespoons	In Cups	In Tablespoons
1/8	2	1/4	More
1/4	4	1/2	than
1/3	5 1/3	2/3	you
1/2	8	1	would
2/3	10 2/3	1 1/3	want
3/4	12	1 1/2	to
1	16	2	measure!

Index

( ) = optional alternative to other grain 16

A

Adding and maintaining air 7
Agar agar 4
Allergen cross contamination 1
Allergens 9
Apple Bread 47
Apple Buckwheat Pancakes 18
Apple Crisp 126
Apple juice 5
Apple Muffins 32
Apple Oat Cereal Muffins 33
Apple Pie 136
Apple Rice Cereal Muffins 34
Apple sauce 5
Apricot 79, 80, 121
Apricot Oat Bars 52
Apricot Oat Trail Bars 53
Arrowroot 4, 5
Athletic Activities 14

B

Ba = barley 17
Baking Basics and Tips 6
Baking powder 2, 5
Baking soda 5
Bananas 3
Banana Bread 41
Banana Chip Cookies 58
Banana Rice Bread 42
Barley 16
Berries 3, 80, 121, 123, 124
Birthday Cakes and Cupcakes 88-95
Birthday Party 13
Blending 7
Blueberry Glaze 124
Blueberry Sauce 124
Blueberry, glazed cake 106
Blueberry Muffins 35
Blueberry Pancakes 31
Blueberry Peach Sauce 122
Blueberry Peach Sauce, vanilla cake 114
Blueberry Pie 137
Blueberry Scokiemuffs 20

GF, GF* iv, 16
Ginger 5
Gingerbread 104, 105
Gingerbread Frosting 119
Gingerbread People 73
Ginger cookies 75
Glaze 124
Glazed Blueberry Cake 106
Gluten Free iv, 1, 3, 16 (also see GF labeled recipes)
Granola 27, 28
Greasing a pan 7

H

Halloween 15
Halving recipes 142
Hamentashen 76
Holidays 10, 15
Holidays, cakes for 101
Honey 5, 6
Hot Fudge/Fudge Frosting 118

I

Ice Cream v, 96-99
Ice Cream Cake 99
Ice Cream Sandwiches 97
Ice Cream Treats 98
Ingredient temperature 6

J

Jam Cookies 68, 79

K

Key of Grains, Gluten, and Sugar 17

L

Lecithin 3, 5
Lemon Cake 107
Lemon Icing and Frosting 119
Lemon juice 5
LNS = little or no white sugar 16
Locate ingredients 1

M

Mango Bread 47
Maple Frosting 120
Maple Raisin Cookies 80
Maple syrup 5, 6
Measuring 5, 6
Molasses 5, 6

Morning play group 10
Muffins iv, 32-39
Muffins, Quick Breads, and Tea Cakes 31

N

Nectarine Bread 47

O

Oa = oats 17
Oatmeal Pie Crust 133
Oatmeal Raisin Cookies 81
Oats 3, 5, 16
Oil 3
Optional alternative to other grain 16
Orange Frosting 120
Orange Raisin Cookies 82

P

Pancakes 30, 31
Passover Cookies 86
Peaches 3
Peachy Passover Cookies 83
Peach (or other fruit) Rice Milk Ice Cream 97
Peach Bread 46
Peach Cobbler 128
Peach Crisp 126
Peach muffins 39
Pears 3
Pear Gingerbread, up-side down 130
Pie vii, 136 - 140
Pie Crust 133-134
Pineapple Cake 102
Play Dates 11
Potato flour and starch 4, 5
Powdered sugar 4, 5
Prune Filling 79
Pumpkin Muffins 40
Pumpkin Pie 139, 140
Purim 15

Q

Qu = quinoa 17
Quantity Conversion Chart 142
Quick Blueberry Waffles 30
Quick Breads 31
Quick Bunuelos 61
Quick Filling 80
Quick Pancakes 29
Quick Blueberry Pancakes 30

Quick Pumpkin Pie 140
Quick Waffles 30
Quick Blueberry Waffles 30
Quinoa 3, 16

R

Raisindoras 55
Rasberry 80, 121, 123, 124
Removing a cake from a pan 8
Ri = rice 17
Rice 16
(R)ice Cream Cake 99
Rice milk 5
Rice Pudding 132
Rich Chocolate Cake or Cupcakes 90

S

Safflower oil 3, 5
Salt 5
Sauces 115, 122-124
School Party 12
School Snacks 11
Scokiemuffs 20
Seeds 1
Sesame seeds 27
Setting up the kitchen 5
Shortcake 111
Snack Bars and Brownies 51
Snowman Cake 108
So = sorghum 16
Soft Chocolate Chocolate Chip Cookies 64
Sorghum flour 17
Soy 1
Soy lecithin 3
Sp = spelt 16
Spelt flour 1, 4, 17
Strawberry frosting and icing 121
Strawberry Glaze 124
Strawberry Sauce 124
Strawberry Shortcake 111
Strawberry Syrup 123
Substitutions 4
Sugar 4, 5
Sugar Cookies/Decorated Cookies 84
Sunflower seeds 27
Super Quick Pie Crust 133
Sweet Cranberry Crisps 56
Syrup 123

T

Tapioca flour and tapioca starch 4, 5
Tea 14
Tea Cake 31
Tea Hee Hee Cake 50
Thanksgiving 15
Thickeners 4
Timing 7
Trace amounts of allergens 1
Trans fat 1
Tree nuts 1
Triple sifting 7

U

Upside-Down Pear Gingerbread 130
Using a blender and electric beaters 6

V

Valentine's Day 15
Valentine's Day Cake 114
Vanilla Birthday Cake or Cupcakes 92
Vanilla Cake with Blueberry Peach Sauce 114
Vanilla Cookies 86
Vanilla extract 5
Vanilla Fudge Frosting 122
Vanilla Icing and Frosting 121
Vanilla Pear Birthday Cake or Cupcakes 93
Vanilla Rice Milk Ice Cream 96

W

Waffles 30, 31
Wheat 1, 4
White flour 2
White Frosting, Creamy 121
White sugar 4, 16
Wholesome Zucchini Carrot Date Bread 48
Whole grain flour 2

X

Xanthan gum 4, 5

Y

Yellow Birthday Cake and Cupcakes 94

Z

Zucchini Bread 49
Zucchini Carrot Corn Bread 44
Zucchini Carrot Date Bread 48